FORCED OUT

Forced Out

Migrant Mothers in Search of Refuge and Hope

Susan J. Terrio

NEW YORK UNIVERSITY PRESS

New York

NEW YORK UNIVERSITY PRESS
New York
www.nyupress.org

© 2024 by New York University
All rights reserved

Library of Congress Cataloging-in-Publication Data
Names: Terrio, Susan J. (Susan Jane), 1950–   author.
Title: Forced out : migrant mothers in search of refuge and hope / Susan J. Terrio.
Description: New York : New York University Press, [2024] |
Includes bibliographical references and index.
Identifiers: LCCN 2023003768 | ISBN 9781479823529 (hardback ; alk. paper) |
ISBN 9781479823536 (paperback ; alk. paper) | ISBN 9781479823550 (ebook) |
ISBN 9781479823567 (ebook other)
Subjects: LCSH: Women noncitizens—United States—Social conditions. | Children of
noncitizens—United States—Social conditions. | Immigrant families—United States. |
Illegal immigration—United States. | Mothers—Central America. | Central America—
Emigration and immigration. | United States—Emigration and immigration—Government
policy.
Classification: LCC JV6602 .T47 2024 | DDC 362.83/9812—dc23/eng/20230202
LC record available at https://lccn.loc.gov/2023003768

10 9 8 7 6 5 4 3 2 1

Also available as an ebook

For my husband, Steve Terrio

CONTENTS

Introduction

The Mouth of a Shark

The violence and corruption that are forcing Central American mothers to migrate make home, in the words of Somali refugee poet Warsan Shire, "the mouth of a shark." Home became the mouth of a shark for Teresa when the principal of her school in El Salvador coerced her into having sex with him and nobody believed that he would do such a thing. Especially when she was fifteen and he was forty-one. After all, he was educated, respected, and lived with his wife and three children. She lived with her grandparents, who accused her of lying until she got pregnant. They scoffed at Teresa's suggestion to call the police. Instead, they confronted him and demanded that he pay her school fees and support Teresa and the baby. When Teresa's daughter was born, he rented her a house and paid the bills but expected the sex to continue. When Teresa declared her independence by finding work and winning a school scholarship, he stalked and threatened her.

Seeing no way out, she left her daughter with her grandmother and headed north on a journey where she nearly died twice—once when she fell from a moving cargo train in Mexico and again when she was abandoned by a smuggler in the Sonoran Desert. Border Patrol agents saved her life and took her to the emergency room but handcuffed her to the hospital bed. Two days later they shackled her and transferred her to an immigration prison where the water smelled foul, the food was awful, and the guards were abusive. On her first day there, they put her in a prison uniform, confiscated her pain meds, and sent her to solitary confinement in a freezing cell. Her offense was violating the prison prohibition against physical contact. She didn't know about the rule and when she saw a friend from home, she ran to hug her.

Teresa thought that she had escaped the mouth of a shark when she passed her credible fear interview for asylum and was released from the prison. She skipped her hearing in immigration court because she didn't have a lawyer and was sure that if she appeared the judge would deport her. She settled in Virginia, brought her daughter Sonia safely over the southern border in just one year, and met a wonderful man. He was from her part of the world, spoke her language, and was a pillar of their church. When she got pregnant, he insisted on getting married. After her son was born, her husband rented a nice apartment for the family. For the first time since she was fifteen she felt safe and loved.

Her daughter Sonia was flourishing in elementary school. In her first year, she learned English, performed at grade level, and was named a class leader. But suddenly she became withdrawn and anxious. Teresa didn't worry because she thought that it was just an issue with friends at school. She was shocked when a social worker from Child Protective Services called to tell her that for months her husband had been sexually molesting Sonia when Teresa worked the night shift. Sonia had confided in a school counselor after learning in sex education class about child abuse. Home once again became the mouth of a shark. Teresa was determined to protect her daughter and to cooperate with a criminal investigation. She assisted police in an investigation that dragged on for two years. Her daughter wrote a letter in English to the judge and described the harm she suffered at the hands of her stepfather. Teresa's husband was convicted of child abuse, given a prison sentence, and deported to Guatemala. Teresa's cooperation earned her a U visa that put her on a path to citizenship. Could she finally hope that this home is no longer the mouth of a shark?

This is Teresa's story, but it could be the story of any mother from Guatemala, Honduras, or El Salvador. Since 2012, tens of thousands of young mothers have sought protection in the United States as rates of extortion and killings by criminal groups soared, the rates of abuse and murder of women exploded at home and in the streets, and the rule of law disintegrated in Central America. This unprecedented exodus represented a significant shift from earlier patterns of migration from that region. Although Central American women have migrated for decades, until 2013, Mexicans made up the vast majority of migrants attempting to enter the United States. Since then, the pattern has reversed. The Central American women who have migrated since then have been relatively young mothers, between eighteen and twenty-nine years of age, single, separated, or widowed; had no or only elementary-level education; and were raising their children with little or no support from a partner. Their children were generally between five and eleven years of age.

Interviews conducted with Central American women by the United Nations High Commissioner for Refugees (UNHCR) revealed that 85 percent of these women faced extreme levels of violence on a near-daily basis. They experienced threats, extortion, and assaults from transnational and local criminal groups operating in their neighborhoods alongside life-threatening and degrading forms of domestic violence at home. The women repeatedly told interviewers that the police could not or would not protect them. Sixty percent reported rapes and assaults to the police but received no or inadequate protection. Forty percent did not report harm to the police because they viewed the process as futile. More than two-thirds sought safety by fleeing elsewhere in their home countries but reported that they still remained at risk for injury or death. Although mothers were poor and needed money, work was not their main motivation for leaving. They left to ensure their own survival and to make a future for their children.[1]

US Immigration Policies

In the twenty-first century a widespread—if heavily debated—consensus has emerged that many migrants, including asylum seekers, do not deserve protections under immigration law or have the right to access public goods like decent housing, safe work, or public education.

Increasingly, destination countries like the United States, Australia, and countries in Western Europe are preemptively barring asylum seekers from entering their territories or are making asylum claims legally inadmissible at the outset without the benefit of a court hearing on the merits of their case.[2]

The unprecedented number of undocumented families and children seeking legal protections have put enormous strain on the entire US immigration system. Those numbers have fueled public anxiety about migrants who are poor, undocumented, and, overwhelmingly, people of color. "Illegals" have increasingly been depicted as a national security threat and racialized as other. They have been accused of stealing jobs, committing crimes, and spreading disease.

In response to migration spikes at the US southern border beginning in 2012, both the Obama and Trump administrations shifted from humanitarian approaches to intensified enforcement and deterrence measures. First, in 2014, President Barack Obama expanded family detention in private prisons—prisons in which due process protections were violated, parents and children were systematically mistreated, and medical care was woefully inadequate. Then, in 2018, President Donald Trump's family separation policy ripped over five thousand children from the arms of their parents by sending parents to jail and detaining children alone, many of whom were under five years old, in appalling conditions in packed, freezing cages or repurposed warehouses. In the same year, the Trump administration ended protection for Central American women seeking asylum. Attorney General Jeff Sessions issued a binding opinion, known as *Matter of A-B*, that excluded domestic abuse and gang violence from the types of persecution that were recognized under US asylum law. These are the very forms of violence that push Central American mothers and children to migrate because the police and the courts in their countries provide no protection.

The Trump administration enacted harsh deterrence policies targeting first asylum seekers and later all migrants. On January 25, 2019, the Department of Homeland Security implemented the Migrant Protection

Protocols, or the Remain in Mexico policy. This required asylum seekers arriving at the US-Mexico border to return to Mexico to await a formal hearing in a US immigration court. Trump's rationale was to limit purportedly fraudulent asylum claims. Given huge backlogs in immigration courts, this policy meant that migrant families seeking protection were stuck for months in squalid tent camps, without enough food or water, and close to areas controlled by Mexican cartels and gangs. Despite this policy, the number of migrant families who fled north and were apprehended at the US-Mexico border skyrocketed from 70,407 in 2016 to 430,546 in 2019. In March 2020 during the pandemic, the Trump administration used an emergency health measure, Title 42, to shut the border to all asylum seekers and to expel families and unaccompanied minors who might otherwise have been permitted to enter. But families continued to come because of the violence back home.

The Biden administration reversed some of the draconian immigration restrictions of the Trump era. It ended mass worksite raids as well as long-term family detention, repurposing the three family detention sites in Dilley and Karnes City, Texas, and Berks Detention Center in Pennsylvania to hold single adults. It closed two notorious immigration prisons, one in Georgia and one in Massachusetts, because of flagrant civil rights violations. And in June 2021, the administration ended the Trump policy that limited asylum for gang and domestic violence survivors.[3] As a result, the average monthly asylum grant rate climbed from 30 percent to 49 percent during 2021.[4] In addition, the Biden administration raised the yearly refugee admissions to 125,000, the highest level since fiscal year 1993.[5] In 2021, lower courts successfully blocked the Biden administration's effort to end the Remain in Mexico policy. But on June 30, 2022, following an expedited review, the Supreme Court ruled in a five-to-four decision that the administration had the authority to reverse the Trump-era initiative keeping asylum seekers in Mexico while their cases are reviewed in US courts.[6] By 2022, the Biden administration had expelled a staggering 1.7 million unauthorized migrants without first permitting their claims to be heard in immigration court.[7]

Because the push factors affecting migrants remain acute, they continue to come. In May 2022, immigration authorities apprehended 239,416 migrants, the highest monthly figure in twenty-one years. Of that number, 165,200 were single adults, 14,699 were unaccompanied children, and 59,232 were families.[8] When home is the mouth of a shark, survival is the only thing that counts.

Why Undocumented Migrant Mothers?

Although I had written two books on the challenges faced by migrant children from Central America and Mexico,[9] I knew little about the plight of migrant mothers in detention until 2017, when I attended an immigration conference at the University of the District of Columbia Law School. For no crime other than crossing the border without papers, they were routinely detained for long periods in private immigration prisons. After apprehension, they were placed in removal proceedings in courts where they had no funded legal representation. One immigration lawyer at that conference described the anguish of a mother who was detained with her children in the Berks County Detention Center in Pennsylvania. Her young daughter had spit up blood for days before the staff allowed her to seek treatment in a hospital. The attorneys described the abysmal conditions in immigration prisons. There was little federal oversight, routine due process and civil rights violations, consistent neglect of medical care, and lasting trauma of incarceration that had no definite end. The attorneys pleaded for volunteers to help them prepare detained mothers for their credible fear interviews, the first step in petitioning for asylum. I traveled to two private immigration prisons in Texas in 2017 and 2018, respectively, where I served as a volunteer legal assistant. I heard the stories of forty-eight women from Central America and Mexico. I also visited mothers who were detained in Irwin Detention Center in Georgia, the state where I now live. That prison became notorious after credible reports surfaced in 2019 that the women detained there were being sterilized without their consent. When they complained, they were deported to the countries they had fled.[10] In contrast, we know relatively little about the undocumented mothers who escape detention and try to build lives in the United States. That is why I began research for this book on the experiences of undocumented mothers.

I focused on mothers who settled in Fairfax County in Northern Virginia because it is one of the fastest growing immigrant destinations in the country. In 2018, the foreign-born made up more than one in four residents in the region. Responding to the needs of this population, public school officials in Fairfax County implemented an innovative program aimed at helping both resettled refugees and undocumented families with children. The program provides assistance with school enrollment, connects families with social services, and hires immigrant personnel in each school to assist new arrivals. They offer free parenting and family reunification classes for immigrant parents who have been separated from their children, often for years, before they were able to bring them to the United States. In 2017, I met the directors and staff of that program.[11] They permitted me to attend the family reunification and parenting classes and introduced me to undocumented mothers who were willing to share their stories. In contrast to the mothers I met in immigration prisons, all but two of the women I interviewed in Virginia had escaped apprehension while crossing the border.

I conducted the interviews in 2017 and 2018. This was a time when the Trump administration drastically lowered the number of refugee admissions, pressured Immigration and Customs Enforcement (ICE) to find and deport all undocumented people in the United States, and reversed protections provided by Temporary Protected Status (TPS) and Deferred Action for Childhood Arrivals (DACA). In a tense environment of enhanced enforcement operations in Fairfax County, these women had to continue to go to work, shop, and get their children to school. They felt the gaping maw of a shark in their communities every time a mother's workplace was raided, she was detained after a traffic stop, or abruptly deported after appearing for a routine check-in with ICE. On days when ICE announced raids or stationed their vehicles outside public schools, their children were forced to hide at home. They knew families whose kids came home from school to an empty house after a parent was taken away. They saw first-hand what happens when a parent is deported. Families are shattered, they face hunger, and risk a plunge into homelessness. Then, their new home becomes the mouth of a shark.

In Their Own Words

This book offers unfiltered, first person accounts of migrant women and children, interspersed with background context and commentary. The stories were told in the women's own language and translated in real time by Ligia Penske Diaz. I took extensive notes in both Spanish and English and later reconstructed the entire interview from the notes. The contextual material and my own depiction of the meetings are included along with the women's life stories in order to provide personal background information and to illustrate important developments in their home countries. I used pseudonyms for all the women and changed some biographical details to protect their identities. That said, the women's stories are reproduced in the way they told them. As a result, they weave back and forth in time as the women remember the decisions they made and what happened as a result. Because the mothers have never narrated their stories in a linear fashion, the dates are not chronological. This broken timeline mirrors the way that memory works.

In each individual's story, we hear the shifting attitudes and complex negotiations of women who reject the violence embedded in institutions and everyday life in their home countries. At the same time, these women struggle with gender ideologies that perpetuate their continued vulnerability and dependence when they are in the United States. Rather than sensationalizing their trauma or dwelling on their vulnerability, the women's stories reveal their interior worlds with their astute critiques, insightful commentaries, and funny anecdotes. We are afforded a window beyond the stereotypes of women who are misrepresented as bad mothers, hapless victims, or clever opportunists gaming a broken immigration system in the United States.

What the Mothers Say

Home is the mouth of a shark when you seek help from a public prosecutor in El Salvador after you witness a gang murder your neighbors and they mark you for death. The prosecutor tells you to go home and pray because he cannot help you. Home is the mouth of a shark when the family farm is failing, your mother needs treatment for ovarian cancer, and the family has no money. You contact a smuggler so you can head north to find work. He will pay for the trip only if you marry him. So you do. Home is the mouth of a shark when you grow up poor in a gang-infested neighborhood in Honduras. You have three children by a violent man who enjoys beating you and promises to kill you. You believe him, leave your children with your mother, and head north. Home is the mouth of a shark when you lose custody of your children after the partner who raped you repeatedly tells the police that you attacked him with a knife. You didn't. You're in the mouth of a shark when gang members abduct your niece or extort money from you. If you are lucky your family can borrow money to pay a smuggler to take you to *el norte*.

Home is the mouth of a shark when gangs operate in broad daylight. They demand *la renta*—extortion money—from bus drivers, shopkeepers, and even school kids who pass through their territory. They are in schools and have killed teachers who refuse to give them passing grades. They troll for new recruits, especially boys to be lookouts first, and then gang enforcers. They want girlfriends as their playthings to dress up and make them feel big. Everyone knows what happens to people who refuse to join or pay. They are kidnapped, tortured, and killed, and their bodies are dumped by the roadside. Gangs are just the public face of corruption. They work hand in hand with local officials, police, and criminal groups.

Things are worse when you live alone or with your mother and children and have no man in the house to protect you. If your father, husband, or brothers are working in the United States and send money to you, the gangs know it and demand that you pay their extortion tax. It is the same if you run a small store or work for a salary. And when you do things that are not "normal" for women—like playing soccer on a men's team—they call you a dyke and tell you to stop or they will rape and kill you.

You have learned never to expect protection from the police or the courts at home. There are laws protecting women against violence but officials in these countries usually ignore them, especially if it involves a husband and a wife. People say that it is your cross to bear if your man mistreats you. If you go to the police for help, they laugh and tell you to go home and have sex to make up with him. If the police do investigate the abuse, they ask you to buy their meals and put gas in their vehicles. If they make an arrest it is for show. They release the man within hours and he comes home ready to teach you a lesson. He tries to control you even after you leave, and refuse to support the children. If you go to court to end the abuse or to get custody of your children the judges almost never rule in your favor.

You never wanted to leave home but had no other choice. You came first hoping to bring your children once you found steady work. Too often it took years before you could afford to get them over the border. You know mothers who brought young children along because there was no one to care for them back home. Some people said that if you made it across the border you would be allowed to stay and even get papers. Many of you knew better than to believe those stories. Who would take such a risk based on a rumor? Everyone knows how dangerous it is to go through Mexico as a woman without money or documents. Women get raped, kidnapped, or even killed. No mother would leave on such a journey alone or with her children if she had another choice. You leave hurriedly without goodbyes or even explanations so you can stay ahead of the shark. You pray to God that you will survive the journey.

So you begin a perilous trek that can last months and cost more than people from your country will earn in a year in the United States. As you head north, the bite of a shark is always threatening. You take buses or taxis, ride on top of cargo trains, and walk though remote areas to avoid immigration officials and criminal groups. At the Guatemalan border, Mexican immigration officials catch you and deport you back to your country. On a second trip, you might make it to Mexico but have no money and must outrun or hide from the authorities and the gangs. It takes much longer that you planned and you must work or beg on the street to survive. Sometimes you get assaulted or robbed. You are scared and often go hungry. If you are lucky you go with guides who can be trusted and cross the border without being apprehended. If you are not lucky, you could drown crossing the Rio Grande, die in the desert, or get caught by the migra, immigration, in the United States. You could get deported or transferred to one of the private immigration prisons where the conditions are horrible and detention can last for months.

You think that you have outrun the shark when you pass a credible fear interview with a US asylum officer in the prison and are released on bond. Then you find out that to get legal status you must appear before a judge in an immigration court. If you don't show up for the hearing you will get a removal order. You don't understand anything about the law in this country. They say that you can have an attorney but only if you pay for one. How? You have no money and they warn you that good volunteer lawyers are few and far between. You have heard that even with an attorney it is very hard to get legal status, especially asylum.

If you make it across the border without being caught by US immigration you think that you have outwitted the shark. You join undocumented relatives in Virginia who help you find a place to stay. You live with six people in a two-bedroom apartment. But you have no papers and have to work long hours at two bad jobs—washing dishes and cleaning houses—in order to pay expenses. You must send money to support the children you left behind and repay the loans you borrowed to make the trip. You promised to bring your children over right away but quickly realize that it will take much longer that you thought. You make so little, expenses are so high, and the smuggling fees have skyrocketed. Years go by before you can bring them over. Even though you have worked and paid taxes in the US for years you are not eligible for legal status. Not now, not ever. You continue to live in the shadows, trapped in a permanent limbo. You make a home with people from home but you are forever at risk of being cast out.

Your children say that home is the mouth of a shark when they have to leave behind the grandmother who took your place after you left. They remind you that they nearly suffocated in the back of a trailer truck on the journey north. They were terrified when immigration caught them at the border and handcuffed them. They didn't understand why agents put them in a cage and sent them to a government shelter when they knew you were here. They feel safer in the US but they miss playing soccer back home with their friends or hanging out with their cousins. When they finally make it here after years of separation, they are angry because they say that you abandoned them. They insist that they didn't really care about the clothes or the school money you sent. They just wanted their mother to be with them. They say over and over that the US is not what they imagined. English is hard, the schools are different, the workload is heavy, and it is tough to make friends. It is full of poor people and tough neighborhoods. Then they stick the knife in. They say that the worst part is that you are always working and once again they are alone at home. Thank God some of the children catch on, begin to learn English, and find a teacher or coach who cares. Will your children be able to call this place home and have a normal life?

After Trump was elected, life got much harder in Northern Virginia where you live. In 2017 you started to live in fear when ICE officers showed up everywhere. Many days you kept your children inside the house because there were ICE arrests outside schools, churches, and the convenience stores where workers wait for day jobs. There were also raids at workplaces, and arrests during check-ins at federal buildings. If you got arrested, ICE would detain you and then kick you out. If that happened, your children might have to return to the country you fled or go to live with other relatives in the United States. Worse still, they might be put in American foster care families.

You hear on the Spanish-language news that some Americans hate immigrants, especially those from Central America and Mexico. They say that their country is being overrun with illegals who steal jobs, commit crimes, and spread disease. They think that you come here to have babies and to game the system so you can get papers. You want Americans to know that you are not a threat. You are not criminals, bad mothers, or helpless victims. You just want to provide for your kids, work hard, and have a chance at a normal life. As long as home is the mouth of a shark, people will leave their countries and try to build lives here. You offer your stories so that Americans will understand why.

How the Book Unfolds

The mother's stories are grouped into three parts. "Leaving Home" explains why they left home and why they deserve protection. "Border Trouble" chronicles how they managed to get themselves and their children across Mexico's heavily militarized southern and northern borders. Despite sometimes undergoing multiple crossings, all but two of the mothers I interviewed escaped apprehension by immigration authorities. "Living in the United States" describes how the mothers attempt to build new families in a country where they have no legal foothold or claim to permanency beside their hopes for their children. Their stories are all different but the one thing they share is a history of hardship and a quest for security.

PART I

Leaving Home

1

Luna's Story

"I Have Rights"

Luna lives in a small rental house in Alexandria, Virginia, with her husband and three children who are nineteen, seventeen, and thirteen years of age. It is just two weeks before Christmas in 2017 and Luna has put up a small artificial tree that is decorated with lights and handmade ornaments. It strikes a festive note in an otherwise sparsely furnished but immaculate living room. Luna's sister, who lives a few streets over, is visiting with her two young children, a two-month-old baby and a two-year-old. Ligia, my research assistant, is with me. She works with the Spanish-speaking families and their children and they trust her. She has arranged the interview and after we arrive, I explain that I am a professor at a private university in the city and do research on immigrant families in the United States. I say that I would like to hear Luna's story in her own words. What was her life like in Honduras? Why did she leave her home and family to come to the United States?

1999

I left Honduras to save myself and to give my children a better life. You see, in 1999, I had an eight-month-old baby girl and a swollen belly with a second child when my dad confronted me about my relationship with the children's father. We didn't live together. He would sleep with me at my parents' house, coming and going when he pleased. That morning, when he left without a word, my father got angry and confronted me. He scolded me saying, "He does not show you love as he should." My mom was also upset and asked, "Why do you accept him?" I didn't love him, but I wanted one family and one father for my children. I thought for their sake that I would see if things got better.

We lived in Colonía la Rivera Hernandez outside of San Pedro Sula in Honduras—a barrio now infested with gangs. We were one of the poorest families and lived in a shack with an earthen floor. The walls and roof were made from scrap metal and scavenged wood. There was no electricity or running water. My mom had to carry water from a well and gather fire- wood to boil water and cook. She washed clothes for other families and made little pastries to sell. Our furniture consisted of one table and we slept on mats that we unrolled on the floor at night. I was so ashamed of that house that on school days I ran ahead of the other kids so they wouldn't see where I lived. There were nine of us and we were always hun- gry. We would get excited when there was a pot boiling outside because we thought that meant a good meal. We were usually disappointed because what my mother put in our bowls was just broth flavored from the bones, gizzards, or feet from chickens.

I finished the fifth grade and had one year of sewing class at a vocational school before I started to work at the local maquila. I was fourteen. We produced clothes from pieces they gave us. Each one of us had a task that we did over and over all day long—we stitched sleeves, hems, or labels. I was happy to have that job. I worked at that factory for six years before I met the man who fathered my children. I was twenty and he was thirty- seven. I had to leave my job during the second pregnancy because the shifts were so long and it was too hard to stand all day. I began to sell bread at a local market with my sister. She was also pregnant and had young kids so we worked side by side. If we sold all our loaves, we would treat ourselves to toasted tortillas and then have the rare pleasure of buying chicken, milk, and bananas to feed our children.

Beginning in the late 1970s, free market reforms in Honduras led to the creation of export processing zones designed to attract foreign invest- ment and provide jobs. Foreign companies operating in free zones pay no duties or tariffs, escape government regulation, receive tax exemptions, and have access to cheap, nonunionized labor. For example, large US companies send raw materials to be assembled by Honduran workers in large plants—maquilas—and the assembled products are then exported back to the United States. Eighty percent of the maquilas are linked to the apparel industry. A majority of the workers are women between the ages of fifteen and thirty-five. Most are poor, have little education, and are single heads of their households. Workers earn low wages, work ten-to-twelve-hour shifts in factories that are generally noisy and poorly ventilated, and struggle with nearly impossible production goals.[1] Despite the drawbacks, most Hondurans desperately want these jobs because they pay significantly more than work in other sectors. By 2018, maquila factories were one of the leading industries in the Honduran economy, employing 167,462 people.[2] Poor women have no choice but to leave school early and to work as market vendors, itinerant farm help or, if they are lucky, to get jobs in the growing maquila industry.

The children's father had a taxi and that is how I met him. He would drive us home after work because it was too far and dangerous to go by foot. One evening I was alone in the car with him. Instead of taking me home he drove to the edge of an embankment and said that he wanted me to be his woman. When I pretended not to hear him, he got angry and threatened me, saying, "If you don't agree to have a relationship with me, I will floor the car and we will go over the edge and die." I had to agree. So I became his woman. Afterward he kept coming to sleep with me at my mother's house. When I got pregnant with the first I wanted to end it but he followed me everywhere and made sure I knew that he had a gun. I didn't want a child from a man like that but it was too late. Later, my mother told me that he had another family and a house. I refused to believe her but in my heart, I knew that it was true. What could I do?

After each visit he would give me two hundred lempiras. It was nothing, the equivalent of ten dollars. He didn't increase it even when the second child came. I told him, "You have responsibilities to your children! That is not enough." He ignored my pleas and continued to have me as he pleased. Then he began to beat me and that too became a habit. When we were together, he would look at pictures of naked women and one day he started to fondle himself in front of the kids. I yelled, "What are you doing? Stop it." He punched me really hard in the face and I ran outside to get away. He grabbed our son, who was only four months old, and he threatened to throw him out of the window if I didn't come back. So I went back in and he hit me harder. Somehow I managed to take the baby and my little girl and we left the house. Another time when he was beating me my father couldn't contain himself. He grabbed his machete and screamed, "Leave now or I will kill you!" He left and did not come back for about a month. When he did, I accepted him again.

As Luna was describing the abuse, her youngest son Chris slipped into the living room where we had the interview. He sat down beside his mother. She turned to him and said, "You know this, right? You have heard this all before." He nodded. I asked Luna if she ever considered going to the police and asking for help. She scoffed and said, "The Commission on the Rights of Women does not function in Honduras. We all knew that. I never went to the police."

* * *

In the late 1990s and early 2000s, successive Honduran governments, under pressure from human rights organizations, ratified regional and international conventions on women's rights. The Congress passed legislation that criminalized domestic violence, rape, and the murder of women. This legislation had little effect on women's lives since law enforcement and the courts consistently failed to enforce it. Public officials actively collude with criminal actors or are themselves perpetrators of violence against the women they are supposed to protect.[3] Police and prosecutors view domestic violence as a family matter and do not intervene.[4]

I got pregnant a third time and I was always afraid. I was always under threat. He knew that I was pregnant again and I heard nothing from him. I went to find him and asked him what I was supposed to do. I got no answer and no support—it was always the same. So I went back to work in the maquila because I had to feed my children. It was the only work available outside the home. By that time the conditions and the pay were a bit better and I worked until my third child was born. The delivery was easy and I was able to buy a crib and a stroller. Then, forty-two days after the birth—that is traditionally when sexual relations can resume—I heard a car outside my mother's house. I tried to hide the baby from him but he just walked right in. He wanted to see if the child was his. He lifted the baby's diaper and said, "Oh yes, that's my boy. Just look at those big balls."

Luna shook her head and gave us a look that said, "Can you believe that?"

If the Honduran police do make arrests for domestic abuse, the abusers are frequently released within hours and return home bent on retaliation.[5] If the domestic violence cases reach court, judges often impose light sentences even when women suffer horrific mutilations and life-threatening injuries. A Honduran man who attacked his wife with a machete, severing her left foot and right leg, initially received a prison sentence for "inflicting light lesions."[6] Given the high levels of impunity and the fear of reprisals, women who do report abuse often withdraw their complaints, choosing instead to go into hiding or to flee the country.[7] In Luna's barrio, physical violence against women went unpunished. It also went hand in hand with psychological abuse, including isolation, stalking, insults, and the use of children as pawns, with threats to kidnap or even to kill them. Another Honduran woman explained, "In my country violence in a couple doesn't exist because women are taught that it's a cross we have to bear."[8] Acceptance of male dominance is widespread. That is, until it reaches a tipping point, as it did for Luna, when she decided to leave Honduras with the hope of later bringing her children to the United States.

2005

When my third child was a year and a half, I couldn't take it any longer. The beatings were more frequent and vicious. More than once, their father said that he would kill me. I was sure that the abuse would end with my death. So I decided to leave Honduras and come to the US. One of my brothers had been in the US for three years and he lent me the money for the trip. My mom agreed to take care of the kids and she made arrangements with a local coyote she knew. The price my brother paid included three tries. I thought that I could work in the US for two years and make enough money to build a house and go back to live in Honduras. The arrangements to leave were finalized but I was still breastfeeding my youngest son. The day I had to leave, the baby was nursing and he would not let go of my breast. It was like he knew that I was leaving. I left at midnight and after five days, I made it to Mexico. Right after crossing the border with Guatemala, *la migra* [immigration] got me and deported me back to Honduras. When I got home I nursed the baby again because my breasts were so full of milk. I stayed fifteen more days and the father of my children came and begged me to forgive him. He knew that I had attempted to go to the US. That time, I just said, "Enough!"

Between 2005, when Luna left home, and 2011, Honduras had the highest homicide rate in the world. The country currently ranks seventh globally for the number of femicides—killing a woman because she is a woman.[9] Ninety-six percent of femicides go unpunished by the law in Honduras.[10] Rising crime and violent death affect everyone, but Honduran women suffer different and more extreme forms of violence. Women endure life-threatening and degrading forms of battering including repeated rapes, sexual assaults, and brutal attacks with baseball bats or machetes. Rape is routinely underreported due to the fear of stigma, retribution, and further violence.[11]

I left a second time and made it to the US border. They put us in a hotel on the Mexican side and while I waited I had a dream that I got deported.

My daughter was crying and berating me: "You got deported again! How did that happen? You promised to send back dolls for me to play with." From that hotel, we crossed into the US. We walked for thirteen hours. I felt that I couldn't do it but that dream kept me going and I was praying the whole time. I said my kids' names over and over. I asked God to help me and to give me the strength to make it. We moved at night and finally we met people with a van. They took us to San Antonio and then Houston. We spent three days in a house arranged by the smuggler waiting for my brother to send the rest of the payment. During that whole time, we never saw the police or immigration. We left from Houston and arrived in Virginia two days later.

When I came in 2005, I began to work at a restaurant washing dishes and cleaning after hours. I remember that I got my first pay on November 24 and I immediately wired money back home because it was almost Christmas and I was so happy to be able to buy food for my mother and gifts for the children. I loved to send boxes of goods, clothes, and toys to Honduras. But I soon realized that I would not be able to save enough to build a house in two years. After three months I found a better job at a food truck and that is where I met my husband. I was afraid of starting a relationship because he is younger—eight years younger—than I am. I could never forget what happened to me back home. I had never had another relationship in Honduras. Finally, I decided that this was a new opportunity.

The months and years went by and we stayed together. We were happy. We had steady jobs and we rented a nice apartment. I called my kids every day until I was able to bring them over. When I called, they would talk to my husband too. They would tell him about school, their friends, and their grandparents. He wanted to be responsible and to be a father to them. He was funny and the kids liked him. They began to call him "Dad" and we decided to get married.

2014

I was separated from my children for over eight years before we were able to be together. In 2014, when my daughter was fourteen we promised her a big party for her fifteenth birthday. We call it a quinceañera and it means that you have left childhood behind and are a young woman. I never had a big party like that so I wanted to buy her a fancy dress with ruffles, lace, and a tiara. I wanted her to feel special and to have a party with music, dancing, and our favorite foods. I told her that I would send the money but she refused to hear it. She said, "No, the whole reason for this party is for you to be here. I don't want the party if you are not here."

So my husband and I decided to bring her over. By that time the Mara, "La 18 gang," as it is known, was getting bolder, and they acted like they owned my mother's house. They would climb on the roof, go in and out when they pleased, and help themselves to our food. They used it as a hideout, stashing their guns and drugs inside. When my daughter turned fifteen, one of the gang members began to notice her. He followed her to school and even to church saying, "Hey little beauty you can come with me." Everyone knows what happens to people who defy the gang or refuse to pay the tax they impose. Gang members recruit teenage girls as their playthings, and if they resist, they are tortured and killed. The Maras caught one of my nieces when she tried to get across the border in 2012. She was only sixteen years old when this happened. They kept her in a house there and took advantage of her for ten days. When she finally got away she was broken inside. Young kids in our neighborhood back home were doing drugs and smoking marijuana openly. It was a terrible environment. We brought my daughter over first, in 2014, and four months later, in early 2015, we brought over the two boys.

Luna's fears for her teenage daughter at the hands of a gang member were well founded. Gang threats and violence had intensified in Colonía Rivera by 2013. An estimated twelve thousand gang members operate in Honduras and recent reports on gang activity in and around San Pedro Sula show that women and girls are increasingly recruited to sell drugs—a development unheard-of in the past.[12] Although intimate partners are the main perpetrators of domestic violence in most countries, in Honduras, gangs and drug cartels are responsible for half of the murders of women. Gendered retribution is a hallmark of these deaths as women are strangled in front of their children, shot in the vagina, skinned alive with machetes, and dismembered. In 2017, 41 percent of the women and girls killed in Honduras showed signs of mutilation, disfigurement, and cruelty beyond what was needed to end their lives.[13]

Since Luna's children left Colonía Rivera, multiple gangs—the Maras, MS-13, and Los Vatos Locos—now compete for control of different neighborhoods. Residents tell of men who are shot point blank in broad daylight or disappear without a trace, daughters of business owners who are tortured before being killed, their dismembered bodies dumped by the roadside.[14] The lucky ones flee, like the Honduran woman whom I interviewed in 2017 in the ICE immigration prison in Dilley, Texas. She and her husband left Honduras after gang members vowed to kill her when she saw them murder her neighbor's entire family. She courageously sought help from a local prosecutor who told her to go home and pray because there was nothing he could do for her. The former Honduran president, Juan Orlando Hernández, exemplifies the intensification of lawlessness and the failure of public institutions. He packed the Supreme Court with supporters, lifted the constitutional ban on re-election, and was allegedly a key player in the drug trafficking industry, accepting huge sums in bribes.[15]

2017

I have been in this country and worked without legal status for thirteen years. When I crossed, I was not apprehended so they have no record of me. I know that I am not eligible for papers but, more than anything, I want my children to be legal. My Latina neighbors really discouraged me from going to immigration court for my kids because they said that we would just get detained and kicked out. I said that I have to follow the rules and obey the law to protect them. I hired an American attorney who went to the family court and got a Special Immigrant Juvenile Status visa for my two oldest children.[16] They are now legal residents and can become citizens one day. I want the same thing for my youngest son. The Virginia court rejected our petition for a juvenile visa the first time in 2016. I don't really understand why it happened, but the attorney is hopeful that things will work out.

* * *

Special Immigrant Juvenile Status (SIJS) is the only immigration benefit specifically created for juveniles and the only form of relief that requires judicial review from both a US state court and the federal immigration agency United States Citizenship and Immigration Services (USCIS). A US state juvenile or family court must declare that the foreign child is under twenty-one years of age and has been abused, abandoned, or neglected by one or both parents. The court must place the child in the care of a family member or a foster family and issue a finding on the harm the child experienced. That court must further find that it is not in the best interest of that child to return to the abuser, either in the country of origin or at the last regular residence in the United States. Once the state court issues an order, the next step is to petition USCIS for a green card and a work permit. Successfully navigating the process requires finding an experienced immigration attorney. It also requires appearing before a US state court judge who is familiar with the SIJS benefit. State court judges in many areas are not aware that they have the jurisdiction to make custody and guardianship decisions for foreign children who suffer abuse.

I have a good life. We rented this house in Alexandria a few years ago and my three children are doing well. I left Honduras to save myself and to give my children a better life. I had no choice because I knew that I couldn't go to the police about the abuse. There was a Commission on Human Rights in Honduras but it didn't protect women like me. That kind of behavior is just normal for men. I was blind then. I only had my eyes opened once I got here. I know now that I have rights and can use them.

Luna was fortunate in some ways. She had family members in Honduras and the United States who helped her flee, provided the means to hire a smuggler, and cared for her children after she left. She met a man from the same region who spoke her language, was a good provider, and became a devoted stepfather to her children. She escaped apprehension at the border and the costly complication of landing in removal proceedings in an immigration court. That was a good thing since she was ineligible for legal status. Had Luna arrived in the United States in 2014 and applied for asylum within one year as required by law, her attorney could have successfully argued in immigration court that she had a well-founded fear of persecution based on her membership in a particular social group: women in violent relationships whose government cannot or will not protect them. Had she qualified for asylum based on the domestic violence she suffered, she would likely have been granted legal permanent residence and been put on a pathway to citizenship.

In 2017, two of her children were on such a pathway after having earned Special Immigrant Juvenile Status (SIJS) based on the abandonment and neglect they suffered at the hands of their Honduran father. In contrast, Luna, her husband, and her youngest son remained subject to removal at any time. That son faced an additional burden in obtaining the SIJS. He had been apprehended after crossing the border, detained in federal custody, and placed in removal proceedings in immigration court.[17] If his petition for SIJS is approved and a green card becomes available, an immigration judge must still terminate removal proceedings. Between 2017 and 2020, some prosecutors and judges in immigration courts were refusing to terminate removal proceedings for juveniles even after USCIS approved their request for SIJS. They cited the Trump administration's enforcement priorities.[18] In addition, the law bars a child who became a legal permanent resident or US citizen through SIJS from ever sponsoring a parent for legal status. So while Luna's children may well gain the protection of citizenship, their mother will remain undocumented. Two cases of sustained abuse and neglect at the hands of the same man had two very different outcomes.[19]

Luna's story also raises the question of how to interrupt a toxic cycle of violence in the Northern Triangle countries that dates back to colonial times. In the modern era, the increased brutality inflicted by criminal groups and corrupt officials occurs alongside and feeds repeated physical and sexual violence at home. Like the rampant gun violence in the United States, attacks against women and girls create forms of trauma that have stubborn half-lives.[20] The damage from domestic violence erodes a basic sense of safety and self while producing warped notions of both family and masculinity. The experience of abuse casts a long shadow over new relationships. Yet one study suggests that the cycle may be disrupted, if not broken, when migrants are educated on human rights and benefit from laws that punish abusers.[21] A majority—54 percent—of battered immigrant women who are raised in households where fathers and husbands have the unquestioned right to wield violence never report domestic violence in their home countries. Those same women show a significant decrease in their tolerance for abuse once they come to this country and learn that it is a crime. Like Luna, the notion that they have rights is a reason to demand them and to seek justice even in the face of community pressure to remain in abusive relationships.

Migration debt and the high cost of living in Northern Virginia ended Luna's dream of building a home in Honduras. Public school support for immigrant parents and children in Fairfax County, Virginia, lightened Luna's burden of living a shadow life. Yet, in 2017, the muscular immigration raids outside schools, workplaces, and even churches increased and the fear of becoming visible to federal agents spread throughout the local community. Everyone knew stories of ICE agents at the door with deportation orders, children returning from school to empty houses, and parents detained at routine check-ins in federal courthouses. Having constitutional rights such as public education for the undocumented and protection from domestic violence is no substitute for the security of permanent legal status.

2

Ines's Story

"I Wanted to Get Financial Support from My Kids' Father"

We gather in a modest two-bedroom apartment in Alexandria in April 2018 where we meet Ines and her eighteen-year-old daughter Isela. Ines lives there with her current partner and two of her children who migrated from El Salvador to be with her. Ines looks haggard and says that she is very worried about her health. Because she has never had health care coverage, she had her first mammogram just a few weeks before our visit. She finally went to an emergency room because she felt a sizable lump in her breast. She is waiting to get the results of a biopsy but the doctor has warned her that the lump is likely cancerous. She insists on going ahead with our interview because she wants to tell her life story.

1997

By the time I was eighteen years old, in 1997, I had three small children and no control over my life. The father of my children swore at me, insulted me, and beat me. I went to live in his family's house when I was fourteen in a town outside the city of Zacatecoluca in El Salvador. At first, his mother was really nice to me. I soon realized that she wanted me as her personal servant. I did all the cooking, cleaning, washing, ironing, and went to the market. I was sick of that arrangement but put up with it for the sake of my children. Then I found out that their father was running around with other women and I decided that I had enough. I just took my kids, our clothes and went to my mom's house. I decided that I would go to the family court to get custody of my three kids. I wanted to get financial support from their father and to be on my own. That way I could leave behind his abuse, insults, and refusal to help his kids.

You have to understand how desperate I was. By the time I turned fourteen I had been living with my grandmother for eight years and I had started a relationship with the man who became the father of my children. He told me that I was pretty and that I had beautiful eyes. I hadn't heard that from anyone else in my life. I was so young and I fell for his line. You see, I didn't have a mother to give me advice. She lived in the countryside with her four daughters and a boyfriend who abused her and molested her children in the middle of the night. I was one of them. I only escaped after I begged my grandmother to allow me to live with her in town. My grandmother got suspicious and asked my mother if I was being abused. My mother scoffed, insisting that it was just my imagination. But she sent me to live with my grandmother anyway. My grandmother's house had one bedroom that we shared. Instead of going to school I had to sell baskets of bread for a bakery-staying out until all the loaves was sold. Sometimes my baskets were empty at 4:00 p.m. and sometimes not until 11:00 p.m. I had a roof over my head and food in exchange for being forced to work.

As it happened, the year that I turned fourteen, I was invited to a birthday party at the house of a local family and I went. I was so excited because it was a new experience. I couldn't believe how much food there was. There was music, and people were dancing. Everyone was nice to me. His mother knew all about me and at one point introduced me to her son. So, of course, I was flattered when a nineteen-year-old looked at me and complimented me. I realize now that I didn't know him at all but he seemed like a good prospect. He came from a family with means and lived in a big house. Then when the party ended, I realized that I was cornered. His mother insisted that I stay with them in the house. She asked me why I would want to leave. She said, "You are safe here. If you live here you won't have to work as hard and no one will abuse you. You will see that my son is a good man who works hard." I didn't know what to do. I was so naive. I asked her if it was normal for this to happen to young girls. She smiled at me and said, "Yes, of course."

What did I know? I didn't have anyone to protect me, to worry about me, to tell me what to do. His mother convinced me to stay and I did but I was so nervous. I understood that she expected me to sleep with her son. At first, he didn't touch me because I had my period. A few more days passed and before we could have relations I got scared and decided to run away. I went back to my grandmother's house and tried to explain to my family what had happened. But rumors had already flown through the town. People were saying that I had sex with him after the party. They were saying that I was his woman. Then my uncle confronted me, "Why did you leave without telling your grandmother? Why did you go to live with that family when you have a home here? You are a slut who will open her legs for anyone." Then he began to hit me and when he was finished, his wife beat me. I was still a virgin but nobody believed me, not my aunt, my uncle, not my grandmother. So that same day they kicked me out.

I had nowhere to go so I went back to my mother in the countryside. I knew how poor her family was but I went to her house anyway. When I knocked on the door her boyfriend wouldn't open it. He said, "We don't have enough food to have you here. If you want to stay, first bring us food." I was so hurt and angry that I left but now I understand how impossible it was for my mother. She had four children to feed.

In Ines's town, gossip played a vital role in preserving the status quo and reinforcing the vulnerability of poor women. A double sexual standard placed a premium on female virginity and virtue while excusing the sexual exploits and accountability of men. It was common knowledge that Ines came from an impoverished family. The decision to leave her grandmother's house ruined Ines's reputation and guaranteed that her family would see her as tarnished goods. Hypersensitive to a further blight on their family honor, her uncle, aunt, and grandmother imposed a brutal punishment on her. Rejected by both her grandmother and mother, Ines had no choice but to begin a relationship that locked her into a subordinate and exploited position in a higher status family. In this small-town world, women actively colluded with men to reinforce their power over younger, more vulnerable women.

I had no choice so I went back to his house. I began to live with him in April of 1993 and I didn't turn fifteen until May of that year. By that time, I was pregnant. Imagine what you would do if you got pregnant at that age? I had to work selling food even with a big belly. Once again, it was forced labor. And her son, the father of my children, was he the way she described? Not at all! Was he hard working? No! He wasn't even working. He was a bum. All he did was go drinking with his friends and then come home to screw me. We fought a lot and the only constants in my life were insults and beatings.

My first baby was six months old when I got pregnant with the second one. I had had a big fight with him and I took my baby to visit my mom. At that time, I didn't know that I was pregnant. I was in a lot of pain and went to a clinic in the city. They told me that I was pregnant. It was not good news because I never loved their father. He was never involved with the kids and didn't care about them. All he did was drink and then he would scream at me and threaten to throw me out and take the kids away if I ever went with another man. Yet the whole time we were together he was the one who chased other women.

His mother had absolute control over me. I had to obey her without any question and work as much as she wanted. If I refused or said that I planned to leave, she too threatened to take my kids. So after the second one was born, I went back to the clinic and got birth control pills. I had no privacy in that house and she would go through my things. She found the pills and threw them away. When I confronted her, she said that she wanted more grandchildren—five to be exact! When I look back, I realize that she did love them. I couldn't forget that in her house I had food, shelter, and clothes. So time went on and two years after the second one was born, I got pregnant a third time.

When their father found out, he got furious and insisted that I get an abortion. He began to punch me and all the while he was screaming, "Why did you get pregnant again? I don't want any more children with you . . .

no more." There you have a perfect example of machismo. He was yelling that he didn't want a third child and asking me why I got pregnant again. Really? As if I could have refused him in bed? As if I had a way to prevent a pregnancy? The beatings and tirades continued. Things got so bad that I went to see a friend of mine who was a nurse and told her my problem. She said that she could give me an injection that would make me miscarry. She wouldn't tell me what it was except to say that it was very dangerous. We both knew that abortion in my country is illegal, especially for a nurse to do it. She warned me that if I ended up with any medical complications, she would deny helping me.

Ines considered getting an abortion during a period when Salvadoran legislators were preparing to institute one of the toughest antiabortion laws in the world. In 1997, El Salvador became one of three countries in Central America to impose a total ban on abortion even in cases of rape or incest. When poor Salvadoran women are victims of domestic violence, they rarely seek redress from the police or the courts because their reports are ignored. Yet if they seek to end unwanted pregnancies, they can be vigorously prosecuted and face long prison terms.[1] The abortion ban is so broadly enforced that even women who suffer miscarriages or stillbirths have been prosecuted for murder and sent to prison. Medical professionals who perform abortions can be barred from practicing medicine and receive prison sentences of six to twelve years. Family members who help women end a pregnancy can also be prosecuted for a crime. In 2018, the president of El Salvador, Nayib Bukele, claimed that he favored permitting abortions to save a mother's life and was totally against criminalizing women who had miscarriages. Nonetheless, his administration did nothing to ease the abortion ban or prevent convictions for miscarriages.[2]

I thought a lot about it. I decided not to go through with it. I decided to have the baby and love him or her no matter what. So I didn't get the shot. When I came home their father knew where I had gone. He said that he was sorry and was glad that I didn't lose the baby. He said to me, "Where two can eat, three can eat. Please don't do this." His mother begged me not to get rid of the baby. In the end, I had the baby. But things didn't improve at all. I remember that when I had the first child, the father came with me to the hospital and stayed for the delivery. With the second he hired a taxi to take me to the hospital and came after the baby was born. With the third, he just dropped me off at the front of the hospital. It was raining and he didn't want to get wet.

By 1997 I was only eighteen years old and had three children. Since I was living the life of a servant I really started thinking about my situation. Since they controlled me I had to think about how to get some independence. I knew that I could get work at a maquiladora. So I talked to my mother-in-law and said, "How about if I wake up early, do all the chores, you take care of the kids and I go out to work?" How could she turn that arrangement down? So I went to work and it was working out well. I got out of that house, made money, and saw other women. But a few months later, my husband saw how well I was doing and wanted to work there as well.[3]

So I got him a job and he worked for a year and a few months as he promised. But one of my friends told me that everyone at work knew that he was chasing other women. There were no secrets there. She said, "How can you put up with him?" I decided that I had to leave and told her to come and get me one day after work. I took the kids and went to stay with my mom. She had left the abusive man she was living with. At that point I had two choices: I could stay with my mom who had four children and one child from her last partner. I had three kids so that meant that I would have to take care of eight kids. They were all so young. Or I could try to get custody of my three kids, get some financial support from their father, and live on my own. I could leave behind his abuse and indifference.

So I went to the family court and explained why I needed help. I thought a lot about what to say and I was well prepared. I described the neglect and the humiliations that I suffered and asked for financial support for my kids. And I won a favorable judgment from the court. That was so unexpected and my husband couldn't believe his ears. He insisted that he couldn't pay because he had no work. The judge told him that he had to pay. He said, "I don't care if you are unemployed, these are your children and you have a legal obligation to provide food and shelter for them. If you don't pay you will go to jail." I was so happy and I couldn't believe it. It was really rare for a judge to listen to a woman like me. But my good fortune didn't last. My husband's family retaliated against me in the meanest possible way. His sister went to the police and filed a complaint, saying that I threatened to kill her with a knife. It was pure extortion. A few days later his sister came to me and said, "The complaint against you will go away if you tell the judge to withdraw the judgment against my brother." So because I was afraid, I went to court and told the judge that I didn't need the court order because he was paying support. His sister was in court that day and asked to take the two youngest children back to the family's house for a visit. When I went to pick them up, they refused to let me in or to see my kids. My husband said, "The two youngest are ours. You will never have them." I was powerless to protest so I took my eldest son and went to live with my mom. My son understood what was going on and he promised that he would never leave me.

Given the response of Salvadoran authorities to cases involving domestic violence, custody disputes, and the failure of many fathers to support dependent children, the fact that Ines sought help from the family court was an act of desperation and courage. In civil courts where these cases are heard, family judges sometimes favor mediation as a way to address abuse and conflict. Such cases assume that the men and women can participate equally in the process. Existing laws underplay the gendered aspects of violence as well as the social norms that require women to submit to men. Judges often focus on keeping the family unit intact rather than recognizing the rights of abused women. Too often, they pressure women to enter binding agreements with abusers that can endanger them.[4]

So my oldest son and I went to live with my mom from 1999 until I left El Salvador in 2005. 2004 was a very difficult year because we were the only women in that house. By then I had met the man who became the father of my fourth child, a daughter we named Isela. He was a good man, who supported me and we became a couple. Soon after Isela was born in 2003, he went back to the US to work. In 2004 the problem was the gangs that were everywhere.[5] They knew that we had a relative in the US and that there were only women and children in the house. Their threats became more frequent and menacing. They would surround the house, put messages under the door, and write gang signs outside. When we went outside, gang members followed us and taunted us. I was too nervous to go out to work and things got desperate. There was no money and I had to go north. So I told my new partner that I was coming to the US with a friend in 2005. It took us three months to get to Mexico.

2005

The most difficult part of the journey was when we got to Mexico. We made it to Ciudad Hidalgo in the state of Michoacán and the guide took us to a small concrete house. Someone had died there and they had just removed the body. There was a terrible odor and there were six of us huddled in that small space because we were hiding from Mexican immigration. The heat was suffocating. We saw where the body had been buried. The dirt was loose and piled in a mound. We had to stay inside that house from 7:00 p.m. to 4:00 a.m.

The other difficult time was after we crossed the Rio Bravo[6] to enter the US. We changed guides often and there were five other women beside me. We were shocked that the guides on the US side demanded to check our vaginas for hidden drugs. The guide took us one by one out of the car to a room where we had to undress. The guide made us sign papers and then he reported to his boss. No one told us about the internal check. We found out later that the guide was killed because he broke the rules.

On December 24, we made it to Houston from San Antonio. We had to walk most of the way and at night. It was over two hundred miles. We went to a house owned by the head smuggler's lover. He had a wife in El Salvador and a lover in Houston. She was a very kind lady. We were in really rough shape after that walk. One man had twisted his ankle. I picked up thorns in my feet and my clothes were filthy. She allowed me to bathe but I couldn't go on to Virginia because Isela's dad had only sent $600. So I stayed in her house until I could continue the trip. He sent money a few weeks later for my trip to Virginia. He paid a total of $5,600 to get me across the border and to Virginia. They picked me up in a van and we took three days to go from Houston to Virginia. We arrived in Virginia at 3:00 a.m. on New Year's Eve. I had great hopes for my life.

I worked six years for a cleaning company and shared an apartment with my partner and seven people before I could afford to bring my eldest son to the US in 2012. By then, he was seventeen years old and grown up but I was so thankful to be able to bring him over. Soon after I saved enough to pay a smuggler to bring over Isela. The saddest part is the two kids who stayed behind in El Salvador and lived with their father's family. I realized the kind of family it was so I stayed in contact and always sent them money. I always took care of my kids but I was never able to raise them.

At this point Ines's daughter Isela, who is home, sits down to share her story with us. She has been in the United States since 2013 and is now eighteen years old. We ask her about how she felt about leaving her country and coming to the United States.

Isela shared her story:
I lived with my abuela [mother's mother] for so long that I considered her to be my mother. One day my cousin came to take me shopping. She told me that we were coming to the US together. When I got back to my abuela's house I started to cry. I had never spent much time with my cousin and didn't know her very well. By that time, it was all arranged with a guide. We left together, moving by car and staying in hotels. When we got to Mexico the guide left me at a small store [bodega] out in the country.

Ines:

I was so afraid for her during that trip. We all know that girls get raped and kidnapped and for that reason Isela's father didn't want her to come to the US. He said, "I won't pay." That is why she had to stay in the bodega in Mexico for four days. I told him that she was stuck there alone but he still refused to pay so I had to borrow the money.

Isela:

The area was near a wide river. When it was time to leave, we crossed the river at night in rubber rafts and saw helicopters flying overhead. Everything was dark and as we neared the other side, someone fell off the raft and nearly drowned. We made it to the other shore. There was high grass, trees, and a swampy area. Some people had to leave behind their bottles of water and we walked for so long. There was a woman with a baby—her granddaughter—and the baby was crying and the woman said that she couldn't walk anymore. Some old man helped her. My cousin had her period and had terrible cramps. We had nothing at that point, not water and nothing for my cousin's period. We passed a house and saw an old lady standing in front. We asked her for help and she waved us away. At one point my cousin said she couldn't go on and she just sat down. I stayed with her. We were in the US at that point and when we saw the headlights of a border patrol truck we just turned ourselves in. They immediately separated us and sent us to different detention centers. My cousin was over eighteen but I was still a minor. I got sent to a government shelter for juveniles.

Ines:

So when she was in custody, I filled out the paperwork [for her release] and they approved it. They told me the day and time of her flight. I had to pay for her ticket and for the ticket of the social worker who escorted her. I wasn't expecting that. When she arrived, she walked right by me. I didn't even recognize her. I left her in El Salvador when she was just two years old and came here. It had been almost ten years since I had been with her. I had pictures but I still didn't recognize her. It was so difficult because she wouldn't hug me. I cried because she didn't want to stay with me, she wanted to go back with the social worker. She didn't know me. She refused to talk to me or to her dad. When I asked her questions, she would just shrug her shoulders. Then as time went on she began to talk little by little.

Isela:

What my mom says is true . . . I just didn't feel comfortable. I missed my abuela so much and I was so sad. Of course, I had seen pictures of my parents but I had never really lived with them. I came five years ago. It was tough in school at first but the ESOL [English for Speakers of Other Languages] class saved me. I made friends there. We sat together at lunch every day. They helped me find my classes and do my homework. All my subjects were in English and Spanish. The kids in ESOL were from Honduras and El Salvador. Now I get mostly good grades.

Because immigration caught me, I had to go to an immigration court. We tried to get a lawyer but none of them called us back. Finally, a lawyer from Ayuda [an NGO in DC providing legal services to immigrants] helped me to apply for a SIJS.[7] I qualified and got approved but there were no visas available. The lawyer said that it is a very slow process and that I have to wait. We have been waiting for two years. My mom has a separate case in the immigration court because of her first husband in El Salvador. We don't know how that will turn out.

Because the Special Immigrant Juvenile Status (SIJS) visa is categorized as an employment-based visa, it is subject to a yearly cap on available green cards by country. Even after receiving approval from United States Citizenship and Immigration Service (USCIS), the petitioner must wait for an available SIJS visa. Beginning in 2016, the demand for green cards for child petitioners from El Salvador, Guatemala, Honduras, and Mexico began to exceed the supply. A SIJS backlog emerged and the wait time for a green card was from two to five years. As of April 2021, forty-four thousand children from El Salvador, Guatemala, Honduras, and Mexico with an approved SIJS have been trapped in a legal limbo. They cannot work lawfully, access medical care, or obtain tuition aid. Worse still, they have no protection from deportation. The backlog was exacerbated by Trump administration policies that sought to delay or deny SIJS petitions.[8] Between 2016 and 2018, immigration attorneys noticed that increasing number of applicants for the SIJS received notices that USCIS intended to deny the petition or made approval contingent on supplying more evidence.[9]

Growing up, Ines experienced multiple forms of violence at the hands of family members ranging from sexual abuse, labor exploitation, and parental neglect to housing insecurity. The violence was inflicted directly through physical assaults and psychological abuse as well as indirectly through the uncertainty of an everyday life of poverty. Her young life was governed by chronic deficits in food, clothing, education, family support, and emotional stability. In a society marked by deep class and gender inequality, she made the only choice available to her. She chose survival.

Ines's attempt to seek justice in a Salvadoran family court initially succeeded, against all odds, and offered her the tantalizing prospect of a measure of economic independence and emotional stability. Yet, in short order, the family of Ines's partner shrewdly managed to sabotage the judge's order. Accusing her of attempted murder was a charge that trumped the failure to provide financial support and forced her to withdraw her complaint. Rather than win custody of her children and leave their abusive father, she lost her two youngest children who remained with their paternal grandmother. The children she chose to have and nurture despite years of abuse are now separated from her. They are part of a transnational family divided by long distances and a militarized border.

I spoke with Ines and Isela in April 2018 during a period when the Trump administration instituted harsh restrictions on immigrants seeking refuge in the United States. Just twelve days earlier, the then attorney general, Jeff Sessions, announced a new "zero-tolerance policy" which criminalized all unauthorized entries into the United States.[10] Intended as a policy to deter Central American and Mexican migration, Sessions briefed US prosecutors on how to handle families arriving at the US border. He told them, "We need to take away the children." In a national speech in San Diego, California, on May 7, 2018, he declared, "If you cross this border unlawfully, then we will prosecute you. It's that simple. If you smuggle illegal aliens across our border, then we will prosecute you. If you are smuggling a child, then we will prosecute you and that child will be separated from you as required by law."[11] Before the practice was officially ended in June 2018 due, in part, to public outrage, Trump's family separation policy had ripped over five thousand children from the arms of their parents. Immigration officials jailed parents and detained children alone, many under five years old, in appalling conditions in packed, freezing cages or repurposed warehouses.

Just six weeks later, Sessions issued a decision that negatively impacted all Central American and Mexican women seeking asylum protection in the United States after suffering domestic or gang violence. On June 11, 2018, Sessions issued an opinion that excluded domestic abuse and gang violence from the types of persecution recognized under US asylum law.[12] The result was a sharp downturn in asylum approval rates, with many people being ordered deported to grave violence in their home countries. On June 16, 2021, Attorney General Merrick Garland vacated the Trump-era rulings that ended asylum protections for gender- and gang-related violence.[13] Lifting the legal impediments to eligibility based on these grounds dramatically increased asylum approval rates.

The attorney general's 2021 ruling reopened the possibility of a positive outcome for asylum petitions for battered women from Central America. Currently, the law imposes a one-year deadline for filing an asylum application but also allows certain exceptions to the one-year filing rule.[14] Yet even if Ines could qualify for a waiver to the one-year deadline for filing an asylum application, she would face significant hurdles in the immigration court in Arlington, Virginia, where her case would be heard. These hurdles include a huge case backlog (up to 1.7

million cases in 2022), hostile government prosecutors, and a system where asylum grant rates vary widely by judge and jurisdiction.[15] Between 2016 and 2021, Arlington immigration Judge Paul McCloskey denied asylum in 93 percent of the cases he heard in contrast to Judge Robert Owens, also in Arlington, who denied only 38 percent. Overall, Arlington immigration judges denied about 55 percent of the asylum cases they heard.[16]

In contrast, Ines's daughter Isela is on a pathway to citizenship. The Biden administration offered additional protection to children petitioning for the SIJS visa in 2022. A new policy provides work permits and protection from deportation to children who have approved SIJS petitions and are waiting for a visa to become available.[17] However, under current law, even after Isela becomes a US citizen, she will never be able to petition for legal status for her mother. Ines will remain undocumented and in her own legal limbo, physically inside the nation but outside the protections commonly afforded citizens.

3

Sandra's Story

"All I Did Was Work"

We meet Sandra in the basement apartment in Alexandria where she lives with her three children and the father of her third child. My assistant, Ligia, knows her eldest child, Luis, because he attends the Fairfax County middle school where she works. She has asked Sandra if we can speak to them both about their decision to leave El Salvador and about their life in the United States. It is just a few days before Christmas in 2017 and we gather late in the afternoon after Luis has returned from school. Sandra runs a day care center in the home and is able to join the conversation since the mothers have already picked up their children. We sit together in their small living room and Sandra begins with her story.

2003

I came to the US in 2003 when my son Luis was three years old and I was not yet eighteen. His father had left El Salvador two years before to work in the US and he sent us money every month. So we lived apart for two years and then I heard a rumor from my family in the US that he had started to date another woman here. I knew it was true when that woman began to call me, insult me, and boast that she was his woman. Around that time, he began to miss sending us the monthly wire transfers. So I had some money saved and decided to come here. It was too dangerous to bring my son with me so I left him with my older sister. When I got here my cousin on my mother's side was waiting for me and she got me a job at a deli. I started to work right away and then got a second job. When I think back all I did was work. Even as a very young child I had to work in my country.

We were a large family. There were seven children—five girls and two boys. We lived near my father's people but several times a year we went to visit my mother's family. When we were there, everyone had to work, even the young kids. We could not play or fool around. One of my earliest memories is carrying water. I was only four years old. My grandparents had cows and chickens and during one visit, when I was maybe seven years old, my grandmother said, "Go catch that chicken and kill it." It should have been my grandfather's job but he was too drunk to move so I had to chase the chicken. All of us kids would have to pick corn, to sell bread, to gather wood, and to haul water from a well. Our pay at the end of the day was a plate of food. If I helped to make soup I would get more meat at the meal.

That pattern of work continued and when I was only eleven years old, I worked for money. I babysat the little boy of a nurse. They paid me the equivalent of twenty dollars per month. By that time, my mother had been dead for two years. When my mother got sick with cancer our father had already taken up with the wife of one of my mother's relatives. Our father would not allow my mother to go to the doctor because he said that he didn't have the money. But I know that it was not true. My dad was doing fine economically. He had a business raising and selling cattle. I was very close to my mom but even at nine I saw that things between my parents were not good. He had women in a number of different places. Before my mother died, the woman he was with came to the house and saw my mother. She asked my father, "Can that skeleton still be alive?"

My mother died in just three months. My father wouldn't let us attend her funeral and right afterward, he left us alone to fend for ourselves. He had been going back and forth from El Salvador to the US and that time when he left, he took his new woman with him. The house where we lived belonged to my father. It had been a school but was empty then. It was across the street from his parents and his sister. They knew how poor we were, that we had nothing, and that we were alone. They would go to buy dry goods and fresh food and not stop to share any with us. The truth is that they ignored us.

Some of our neighbors were good to us but they were busy with their own lives and we couldn't count on their help. So we had no regular source for food. Luckily we lived in the country where there were fruit trees. We gathered the fruit and survived on that. We also had a chicken and later my oldest sister got a job in another town. With the money she earned she bought a goat so we would have milk. When I left to work as a babysitter my little sister had to watch our five-year-old brother. She was nine and could be on her own. My little brother's task was to milk the goat. That is the way it is in my country. Life is really hard and kids have to grow up fast. For instance, my little sister had to carry buckets of water because we had no running water. She also had to carry wood. For us that was not child abuse. It was just necessary given the situation. After my father left we got ourselves up and went to school. We went in dirty clothes, clothes that were wet. We didn't have shoes, only open sandals that constantly fell apart and we had to fix them with string. After a while we had to stop going to school. We had no parents or relatives to help us so we had to help each other.

My father came back home when I was thirteen. We were managing on our own but he took us all and forced us to live with one of his cousins. It turned out that it was a new family to abuse us. They made us do all the work and beat us. So one day we made our escape. We walked for two days back to the abandoned house. We were in bad shape from the hot sun and lack of food. We carried our younger siblings and one of our young cousins even came with us because he said that he was planning to run away. My father took dogs to track us. When he found us, he beat us and accused us of kidnapping our young cousin. That day he whipped me so hard that it opened a large wound on my arm. It was really bad. I had had enough and refused to return to that house. So I ran. He started to follow me and I threw stones at him and then finally he stopped following me. I got lost and wandered around in the woods alone for twelve days. That is when I met my boyfriend—Luis's father—for the first time. I was starving and he helped me.

So at fourteen I went to live with Luis's father. He was working so I was able to help my sisters and brothers. I would bring them beans and eggs. My older sister was working and she helped us too, but then my father decided to sell the house where we were living and he took the little ones to live with him and his sister. There was abuse of the kids in their house as well. My oldest sister would give the kids money but my father would take it away. How long did that mistreatment go on? I don't know, but it seemed like forever. My sister and I decided to try to take the kids back and raise them ourselves. We even called the local police station and asked if we could do it but they told us that we were not old enough. The law in our country is not good.

2003

So I came here to the US and my journey took twelve days. My godfather connected me with a smuggler that he knew and trusted. During the trip we were not mistreated. It is funny because our smuggler gave us good food—chicken and rice—and plenty of water. Compared to what I experienced in my childhood I ate better during that trip than I ever had. When we were in Guatemala we stayed in a hotel and I got to eat hamburgers for the first time. It tasted so good! My trip was mostly an adventure in part because I traveled with a good friend from home. We always stayed in the front of the group of migrants. The other women and girls in the group had issues with the men but we didn't waste any time with them.

The trip cost $6,500 because it was so dangerous. To pay the smuggler, I used my small savings and borrowed money from relatives in the US. We heard that there were traffickers everywhere. We paid once we arrived in the US. Things have changed since then. Now you give one-half when you start and the other half when you arrive. After crossing we got to a house in Arizona and it was a big operation. There were about 150 people. They split us up and moved some of us from Arizona to LA. When we got there, we had to change our appearance, specifically our hair color. The smugglers gave us an ID and they asked us to do our nails and hair so we would be presentable enough to travel by air. Before we left they took us to a pool so we could get a little tan.

I spent twelve days in LA and worked for a couple from Guatemala. I took their son to school, cleaned and cooked and they gave me money that

I sent to my sister for my son. I was not mistreated. I spoke to Luis twice during that visit. They gave me phone cards to call him and took us out to a Mexican restaurant the night before we left. They bought us new clothes. The idea was to create a new look because we were going to travel by plane. They gave each of us a purse and told us to buy an English language newspaper. Once we were in the airport they told us to walk straight and fast without stopping. We were just amazed at the surroundings because it was the first time that I had ever been in an airport. During the flight they told us to keep the newspaper in our lap and to pretend to be asleep. If the flight attendant asked us what we wanted, they told us to just say coffee. We flew to New York and a cousin on my mother's side was waiting for me.

My cousin got me a job at a deli and I also worked a second job at a fast food place making fried chicken. I learned so much about food there and at first made six dollars an hour. All I did was work. I have had so many jobs. I found work cleaning houses after I moved to Virginia. I made twenty dollars a day, and then I found another job making sixty dollars a day. I got a second job as a waitress at a bar and that was bad because I had to deal with drunks who couldn't keep their hands to themselves. I didn't like that, so next I worked cleaning offices in Crystal City for seven dollars an hour with a company run by Latinos. After that, I met a lady in Annandale who saw my work and paid me eighty dollars a day. Later, a cousin of Luis's father found him a job remodeling bathrooms and got me a cleaning job that paid eighty-five a day. When the work ended that same cousin found me another job going into DC and Virginia where I made really good money. I was paid twelve dollars an hour.

Now I work from this apartment in Alexandria where I provide daycare. I take in three or four kids under school age and am happy to work from home. I have lots of toys for the kids, a small table for them to sit, and I have cots set up in one of the bedrooms for them to nap.

The labor force participation of foreign-born residents in Northern Virginia has long exceeded that of the native born. Immigrants, particularly the undocumented, work at high rates in critical sectors that keep the region functioning. They are workers in grocery stores, utilities, transportation, public safety, manufacturing, and construction. Immigrants fill significant gaps in the US economy. They work as maids, cleaners, cooks, drivers, health care workers, and child care providers. Their workplace contributions, particularly in critical healthcare industries, help keep Americans safe, healthy, and well-fed. Yet immigrants are some of the most vulnerable residents. They make up just over one-quarter of the population but represent 65 percent of those without public or private health care coverage.[1]

So what happened with Luis's father? When I was in New York he called and arranged for me to be with him in Maryland where he was working. When I arrived, things were good for a while until I got pregnant for a second time. Luis's father was not at all happy about that. He and his friend took me to a clinic. I didn't realize why at first but then I realized that it was to get an abortion. What kind of brains do men have? If men have a partner they should love and protect them. They should support them and their kids. How can they act like that? Living with him I saw that he had changed. He had started to drink just like my father when he began to mistreat us.

I asked myself why, because my father used to be a good man. He was very intelligent and when he was younger, he established an educational program for the kids in our town. He taught them how to take care of the environment, how not to litter and pollute, how to keep down mosquitos which cause illness. He taught health education and about vaccines. But when he was older he changed. He began to drink and treated his family very badly. My mother was a good woman and she was very intelligent as well. She helped in the local communities and although she did not have any formal education she learned on the job. Because many of the women were separated from their husbands who were away working or had migrated to the US, she would teach them how to treat every day medical problems and how to take care of themselves and their children.

So after I lost that baby, I left Luis's father and came to live with my aunt in Virginia. That was really difficult because there was no bedroom for me.

I had to sleep on a sofa in the living room and for that I had to pay $150 a month. After a long day of work cleaning I came home and had to cook for the whole family. On my day off I had to take care of her kids. I realized that they wanted to control me and to get the money that I earned. I left that house and went to live with another relative. I cannot feel happy about those memories. All of my family is in the US now and they live in Woodbridge, Virginia. They never gave us love and as a result I cannot bring myself to love them.

For a while people in Luis's father's family helped me to find work, as I said. At one of my cleaning jobs, I met my second partner. He is from Honduras and was working as a contractor. So I started to live with him, got pregnant, and had my second son, Christian, in 2006. The problem was that his father was always going back and forth from Honduras to here. He never helped me, never contributed money for the rent or food. I was working, paying the bills, taking care of my son and then I developed serious foot problems. I had to have surgery and Christian's father was not there to help me. I found myself alone again. Luckily my siblings were there for me.

I met my third partner years later. We were married in a civil ceremony and he is the father of the daughter who was born in 2014. My kids get along well with my husband. They respect him and like him, maybe even more than they like me. When Luis got here in 2016, my husband even took him to school.

In a pattern that carries over from El Salvador, immigrant women in the United States often have multiple intimate partners. As a result, children living in one household headed by a mother may have different fathers. When a relationship ends, the cultural expectation is that children stay with the mothers, who provide the care. Fathers frequently stop supporting their children and may drop out of their lives entirely. Paternal irresponsibility is normalized by gendered ideologies that view men as unable to remain faithful to one partner. Marriage, too, has flexible meanings. Women who live with men who father their children may use the term "husband," but this does not imply a formal contract. Sandra, like other women we will meet, has had children with different partners. When the sexual relationship ended with the fathers of two of her children, they stopped supporting or contacting them. Sandra's situation is different in that she officially married the father of her third child.

2015

At this point, we asked Luis to tell his story.

Luis:

When I was little, we never thought of having to leave home to come to the US. I lived with my mother's sister, her husband, and my three cousins, all boys, in a village outside the town Candelaria de la Frontera. My uncle was a teacher and taught school in a different town. He could only come home on the weekends and we were alone during the week. He was the one who said that it was time for me to come here. Gangs started to show up at the farm and to pressure my aunt and uncle for money.

Sandra:

When Luis was little, I wanted to bring him to the US but he was happy in El Salvador. He was living with my sister and her husband and their three sons. They lived on a dairy farm with cows, a stable, and a corral. They managed because they had workers from Nicaragua who came to work. Luis loved that farm and would help the workers to milk the cows and bring them back to the corral at the end of the day. Plus, he did well in school. But in 2015, everything began to change. Gangs in El Salvador were becoming a really big problem.[2] One of Luis's cousins joined a gang and wanted to recruit Luis. That cousin was in jail in 2015, but he still had gang members come to the farm and threaten Luis.

Luis:

I went to a local school until fourth grade and then I had to take a public bus to a different school in town. I finished ninth grade in a secondary school and did one year in a vocational school. By then, the gangs were a bigger presence and it was too dangerous to be in that town. Gang members rode the same bus I took and they killed someone on that bus. I could not always tell who was in a gang. My mother knew a man in the US who went back to his hometown in El Salvador. He was working as a hairdresser and got killed by the gangs. There was another man who went back and forth between El Salvador and the US. He used to bring supplies to the farm and the Maras killed him. At that point, we decided it was time for me to go to the US.

Sandra:
I don't understand the politics in Guatemala, Honduras, El Salvador, or Nicaragua. The politicians enrich themselves and do nothing for the people. People leave because of extreme poverty and the violence. The government in El Salvador does not do anything about gangs. The gangs threaten people who work or who go to school. If they ask you for money you have to give it to them or they will kill you. If you don't have the money to pay them you are dead anyway. Gangs target small street venders who sell pupusas. If you don't give them what they want, they will hold your hands down on a hot griddle.

Luis:
My dad went back to El Salvador in 2010 with his new family, a wife and two children. His whole family went to the airport to pick him up. I went too and spent a month with his family—his parents and my younger aunts and uncles. They live in Corriento, a very isolated town close to the Honduran border. I rarely saw my dad and after that month, I never heard from him again. I never really knew my dad's parents but was really close with the relatives on my mom's side. My parents each have kids with a different partner but I am the only child from the same mother and father.

2016
So I talked with my aunt and uncle about leaving, but I made the decision to come on my own. It is easier when the young person makes the decision

to leave. The trip north was really hard. It lasted almost fifteen days and I traveled by truck, van, and taxis through Guatemala before crossing into Mexico and then taking a route through Tabasco state to the capital city of Villahermosa. We stayed in a house for five days and slept on the floor. The guide gave us a cell phone and I called my mom every day. The worst part was hiding in a tractor trailer that was outfitted to hold eighty people. It was an enclosed space with three rows and we had to stand up. With only one vent in the roof and no windows it was really hard to breathe. We were in that truck for twenty-five hours from Villahermosa to Mexico City with no bathroom or water breaks and I had nothing in my backpack to eat or drink. From the capital city we took a big bus to Monterrey and headed north to Reynosa on the border. We crossed the Rio Bravo in a small boat but the migra caught us right away. I spent time in a shelter and then they flew me from McAllen, Texas, to Washington, DC.[3]

When I arrived, it was really weird to see my mom. When we got to the apartment I felt so strange. I didn't want to leave my room. I didn't know anyone in my mom's living room, not my stepfather, not my younger brother who was twelve and not my baby sister who was three months old. They were really nice to me. We took walks outside and then I began to play with my brother and sister.

I miss school in El Salvador and I miss my cousins, the cows, and the chickens. There was a longer school day there and I felt like I was learning more there. The pace in the English to Speakers of Other Languages classes here is slower. In high school, I want to change my elective from piano to computers. My mom sent me a computer that I used back home and I want to learn more. The subject that I like the most right now is history. We are learning about ancient Rome, the cities and the government. At first, I didn't know the school system and there were too many papers, too many deadlines. I got lost but now I see that there are a lot more options here than there. I don't know if it will be possible to go to college because it will be really expensive. At school I only have Latino friends from El Salvador, Honduras, and Bolivia, no American friends. I also have a friend whose parents are from a country near Russia, I can't remember the name. They are diplomats and they speak in English. And I also have African friends. What do I do after I get home from school? I don't leave the house. I don't like to be out. I never liked to go out after I got here.

It is late by the time we finish the interview. Luis's stepfather comes home and goes directly into his bedroom without acknowledging us. Sandra, meanwhile, leaves on an errand and returns with a bag of piping hot pupusas for Ligia and me to take home. After I drop Ligia at her apartment in Tyson's Corner, the Capital Beltway is gridlocked. The drive to Maryland will be at least an hour and I am so hungry that I dig into the delicious, hot food.

2018

By the time we schedule a return visit, it is April and spring has arrived in Washington. The cherry blossoms are in full bloom on the mall and children are kicking a soccer ball in the sunshine in a grassy area in front of the apartment building. Sandra's young daughter is playing at our feet and occasionally asking her own questions. She and her half brother Christian are US citizens. Sandra continued her story:

As soon as Luis came, we hired a lawyer to help him get legal status. I worry about him because he is the only one who was not born here in the US. When we met with the attorney, she explained about the juvenile visa and said that we would have to show that Luis had been abandoned by his father. She said that everything that happened in El Salvador had to be put in writing including the threats from the gangs and from his cousin. We had an appointment in the Virginia family court to file a petition for the SIJS. We had to show it would not be in his best interest to return to El Salvador. We had to prove he was reunified with me, was attending public school, and lived in a stable home. The judge was very pleased that we brought his school records and report cards to show her. So the petition was filed and we have to wait for six to twelve months for the decision on the petition.[4]

This president [Donald Trump] terrifies me. He wants to kick us all out. Doesn't he know that we are just looking for a way to survive? Right now, I don't watch the news, I don't watch TV. I can't believe the stories about the separation of families. People in my situation are just surviving. We send money to our relatives there because in our country, there are no jobs and gangs are everywhere. The politicians don't do anything. Life here is good and safe. There are lots of people who come with the idea to work, to save, and to buy a house back in El Salvador and return there to live. That is not our idea. We want to stay here and to make a life.

Under directives from the Trump administration in 2017, Immigration and Customs Enforcement (ICE) significantly expanded immigration enforcement in the county, arresting undocumented immigrants at workplaces, outside schools, in their homes, and during mandated check-ins with federal agents as part of their immigration cases. This was a significant change from previous county policies that had taken a relatively progressive approach to the undocumented population. Public officials came under increased pressure from the Trump administration to crack down on all immigrants, particularly those with pending removal orders. In April 2018, tensions erupted between the democratically controlled Board of Supervisors in Fairfax County and the leadership of the ICE regional office. One source of contention was a 2012 agreement between the county and the federal government. County officials had agreed to cooperate with federal authorities in holding undocumented immigrants in jail until ICE agents could take custody and begin deportation. Until 2017, the county turned over very few immigrants to ICE. That number doubled in 2017 and many residents demanded that county officials resist the harsh enforcement policies of the Trump administration. Some groups complained that the visible presence of ICE sent the message that all immigrants are criminal. They wanted "ICE out of Fairfax." Responding to public outrage over the muscular raids, shattered families, mounting collateral arrests (people picked up during an unrelated immigration investigation), and attacks on sanctuary cities, Fairfax County sheriff Stacey Kincaid canceled the 2012 agreement. She also barred federal immigration officials from participating in discussions about the arrests of undocumented immigrants.[5]

Young immigrants and public school staff were deeply affected by Trump's enforcement policies and his anti-immigrant rhetoric. A persistent motif in scripted Trump speeches since 2015 had been that "immigrants are coming over the border to kill you."[6] The former president described immigrants as rapists, savage killers, predatory gang members masquerading as unaccompanied minors; as animals who cut people into little pieces; and as an invasion force bent on violently breaching the border.[7] His mantra was to build a "big, beautiful wall" to keep them all out.

Sheila Gotti is an ESOL (English for Speakers of Other Languages) teacher who was in her tenth year teaching in a Fairfax County middle school when we met in April 2018.[8] She speaks Spanish fluently and has a graduate degree in Spanish and English as a Second Language (ESL) pedagogy. Most of her ESOL students migrated to the United States from Central America and Mexico, arriving in large numbers beginning in 2013–14. She sees clear signs of post-traumatic stress disorder (PTSD) in her students. "They are on an emotional rollercoaster. Some express rage, sadness, and breakdown and cry. In many situations, for new students especially, [the emotional distress] is too much to handle and they shut down. Others get hyper excited, and act crazy like they are on a high and then come crashing down. Even small noises will startle them and they will jump and react in ways that are not normal. The concern and worry for what might happen to their parents is a constant."

Ms. Gotti related an incident that shows how violence had been normalized in the lives of young people. "Last Friday, in class, there were two boys playing with rubber bands and I was listening to their conversation in Spanish. One of the other boys in class asked, 'What are you doing?' The boy put the rubber band on his arm and said, 'Did you know that if you get shot and really start to bleed, you could use a rubber band as a tourniquet and it could save your life?' He said it so nonchalantly like there was absolutely nothing strange about the conversation."

Unlike many middle school students who have little interest in civics, ESOL students get really engaged with politics. When Ms. Gotti introduced a unit on the Supreme Court case Brown v. Board of Education, her students were fascinated. "They don't know the history of segregated schools and the Jim Crow South. They don't know anything about the racial past of the US. After that unit, and last year, the kids made a bigger connection with it. They were paying more attention to racial strife and they wanted to learn more. They ask really tough questions. The worst day for me was the day after the 2016 election when Trump won. All the students were so confused about why it happened and they asked how it could happen. They all felt rejected and they were all gathered together. They asked, 'Why don't they want us here? Why do they hate us? We are not in gangs. We are trying to get away from gangs.'"

She shared a letter that one of her students wrote to Donald Trump in 2017:

Dear Donald Trump:

I am a student from Virginia. I want to tell you that immigrant people are not criminals as you said. They come to this country to get a job. They are running away from gangs to save their lives and of their family also. Mr. Donald Trump, the border wall is stupid idea 'cause people don't care how big is that wall. They care about the love of their families. Please don't do that. Protect them because a dream is more big than that stupid wall. Please don't be mean. Be kind with everyone and don't be a racist.

Sincerely,

Anonymous

PART II

Border Trouble

4

Isabel's Story

"I Married a Smuggler"

We meet Isabel at a Denny's restaurant on the Richmond Highway in Alexandria. She has to keep a low profile because of her legal status. Meeting her at home was not a possibility.

2002

The story of how I came to the US the first time began in 2002 when my mom came home from the hospital. The year before she was diagnosed with uterine cancer. I was really close to my mother because I grew up with her as a single mom. My three older brothers and my father had gone to the US to work. I was only eight months old when my father left and he didn't come back to see me in El Salvador until I was twelve years old. My brothers stayed in the US because they had status to work.[1] We owned land and farmed for a living. When my father returned, he taught me how to cut and dry the grass to make hay, how to turn the earth over with a plow, how to plant seeds, and when to harvest. We owned cows, oxen, and planted corn. Recently I found a picture with the neighborhood children harvesting corn on the farm. In our tiny canton, Las Mesas in the department of St. Miguel, everyone was related.

One day when my mom was working in the fields, she fainted. When I found her, she had hemorrhaged and was covered in blood. It is hard for you in the US to believe that we had never been to the doctor's even for a physical but it's the truth. El Salvador is a country where most people don't have access to clinics much less to a doctor. We didn't have a car, so my dad called one of our cousins in town to get her help. They came and three men carried her to the car in a hammock. The road to town was unpaved and full of ruts and the jostling caused her great pain. A medical team in the clinic examined her and found the cancer. The doctor told us that the cancer was incurable but to keep her alive she needed a blood transfusion. So they took her to the hospital and it turned out that she needed three transfusions a week. It was incredibly expensive and to pay the medical bills, my father had to mortgage the land he had bought with money he earned in the US.

So in 2002, my mother was at home but she was very, very sick. My dad came back from the US to be with her as much as possible. I was eighteen and he was sending me to town alone to sell wood to make some extra money. Once when I was there I met a young man. I knew right away that he was an outsider but I had no idea why he came to our little town. People said that he was a Mexican coyote who took people up north. At that time, I didn't even know what the word coyote meant. I caught him looking at me as I was stacking heavy piles of wood in the oxen cart. He came over and we introduced ourselves. He had a funny look on his face when he said, "Please don't be offended when I ask you this question—but are you a lesbian?" I was shocked and said, "Why would you ask me a question like that?" "Well," he replied, "you are doing the work of a man." I saw him three weeks later in town and he asked if he could accompany me home. I was aghast. "What are you thinking? That you can come to my house? My dad will kill you."

A few weeks later I was in town and he was there. That time he insisted on coming back to the farm with me. My dad saw him and got really angry because I was his little girl and he wanted to protect me. "How do you know that man sitting out in the cart? Tell me!" I said, "He comes to town every so often. He is related to the Chavez family." We knew that family. But my dad scoffed and said, "He is only interested in getting into your pants." But the man didn't back down or get upset. He looked at my father and said, "My name is Manuel and I am Mexican." As if they couldn't tell! He was dressed like some cowboy from the rancho, with a huge sombrero, a concha belt with a big silver buckle, and alligator boots. He asked my dad about the land, farm work, and expressed his concern for my sick mom. When he was in town, Manuel came by the house regularly to visit. That went on for two and a half months and then he broached the subject of marriage. He wanted to marry me and asked for my father's blessing.

It was complicated with my dad. You see when my father came back to El Salvador he wanted to be close to me but he was a stranger and I didn't feel close to him. He would say, "If I hadn't sent money, you and your mother would have starved." I would tell him, "You weren't here when I needed you. I didn't care about the money you sent." My mother scolded me, insisting "He is your father." "No, he's not," I said. "Uncle Mario"—my grandfather's brother—"is my dad." My dad was jealous of Uncle Mario and sad about the missed years. He wanted to assert his authority as the father. So when Manuel asked my father for his permission to marry me, he didn't answer. Instead, my father took him to the corral and said, "If you like my daughter, there is one test that you must pass. With this lasso you must rope a steer. If you fail this test you cannot marry my daughter." He pointed to one of the young steers that had never been roped and was really fast and skittish. When Manuel approached the corral gate with the lasso, all the steer began to scatter and run. I couldn't believe it and said to my dad, "What have you done? He will be gored." So Manuel climbed the fence, jumped in, and ran around and around after that animal. He threw the lasso again and again but he couldn't do it.

So we didn't get engaged. I didn't really care for Manuel as a future husband. But he was persistent. When he was back in town he kept visiting us and he would bring a basket of fruit or flowers for my mother. He won her heart that way. She told me, "That man is meant for you. Don't let him go!" A few weeks later, we had to take her back to the hospital and we just didn't know how we would pay the medical bills. Since my father had a visa to go back and forth, he decided to take her to the US to get medical care. You see, my two brothers were working in the US and she could stay with them. We got her a travel visa and she went north.

2003

A few weeks after my mother left for the US, Manuel came by the farm and asked why I was so sad. My dad was worried that we would lose the land because of the debts he took on. Manuel suggested a solution: "I will take you up north so you can work." I asked, "Why? How?" He said, "I will pay all the costs for the trip upfront and then you can repay me when you get there and start to work." When I thought about it, I realized that I didn't know him at all. Where would the money come from? Why would he do that? This was the end of 2002 and while I was still considering it, he went ahead and advanced me the money. Manuel told my dad to go the bank and see that he had deposited $3,000. The only catch was I had to use it within six months. In early 2003 Manuel returned and asked if I made my decision. I wanted more time but he insisted that I had to decide. So I agreed to go with him. But there were so many things I worried about. I knew about the horrible things that happen to women on the way up north. I was putting my life in his hands and at night when I couldn't sleep I wondered if he would take care of me or take advantage of me. I prayed a lot about it.

So the plan was for me to leave on a Friday in January. But you see, I didn't tell anyone. Then I got an unexpected call from my second brother in the US. His mother-in-law had died in a car accident in the US and he was bringing her body home to El Salvador. He wanted me to pick him up at the airport the day before I was scheduled to leave home. How could I leave my dad? Finally, I called my mother in the US and told her about the plan. She was so happy because she thought that if I married him I would be taken care of. She knew that she could die at any time.

I went to meet my brother at the airport but we couldn't claim his mother-in-law's body until 1 a.m. It was very late when we returned. I was a wreck because I knew that I had to be in San Salvador the next day by 10:00 a.m. I told my brother that I couldn't attend the burial the next day because I had too much to do. So I packed as quickly as I could and early the next morning I caught the bus to the capitol. The plan was for me to go to Guatemala. Manuel had sent the instructions along with an ID. At that time in Central America there was an agreement that allowed people to travel between countries without having to show a passport. For that reason, I was able to go by bus to Tecun Uman, a town on the border between Mexico and Guatemala. Manuel gave me the address of a hotel and reserved a room in my name. It was a suite. He told me to call him as soon as I arrived and to stay there until he could join me.

With that time on my hands, I thought, "What am I doing here?" I am a simple girl from the countryside. I don't know anything but my farm and village. Should I just go back home? The next day he arrived at about 10:00 p.m. I was so afraid and thought, God help me, now I am at his mercy. So because the city was in a transit zone the stores were all open and we went out. He asked, "What do you need?" I didn't know what to say so he took me to get a manicure and a pedicure. Then we went to a beauty parlor to get my hair done. He looked at me, surprised, and said, "What a change!" It was true I was completely transformed. Then he announced, "Now we go to dinner!" It was a really elegant Mexican restaurant. I looked at the table and saw so many utensils and I didn't know which one to use so I just sat there. I was so nervous and he said, "Relax. You are a lady now. Come on, eat!" There was music and it was very romantic and people were dancing and he said, "Will you dance with me?" I didn't know how to dance but he insisted and led me to the dance floor. He whispered, "Put your arms around me and tell me I am the person that you love." Well, from that moment on, I knew exactly what he wanted. I thought that my father had been right about him all along. I was so worried about what would happen when we got back to the hotel. What would this royal treatment cost me? I was not in love with him and, besides, I was exhausted.

At the time that Isabel left home, Tecun Uman was well known as a transit city in the southern state of Chiapas where an increasing number of Central American migrants crossed into Mexico and took their chances riding atop the cargo trains that ran north to the US border. Isabel was well aware of the dangers she faced as a young woman migrating alone with a coyote: extortion, kidnapping, sexual assault, and even murder. Despite his stated intentions, Isabel was afraid that Manuel might, after all, be a macho Mexican flaunting his power—from installing her in a fancy hotel and dressing her up for a night on the town—in exchange for sex.

We didn't get back to the hotel until 2:00 a.m. When we were in the lobby, he said, "Look I am bringing you back safe and sound." Then he walked me to my room and left me there. His room was next door. I was so relieved that he didn't insist on more than that. I fell asleep and it wasn't until 11:00 a.m. that he knocked at my door. He gave me very precise instructions. He said, "You will stay in your room until 7:00 p.m. tonight. A guide will meet you here and take you across into Mexico. Then you will practice how to speak as a Mexican." He told me not to worry.

So the next day the guide came and I did go with him. Our destination was a town in Mexico called Tostala. We drove all night and arrived there at 6:00 a.m. He got me a hotel room but I was only there for about five hours before another guy came. His job was to take me across the whole country. I was with him for about five days. We arrived in the border town Matamoros and Manuel was waiting for me.

Like most of the coyotes described in the women's stories, Manuel was well known to the local families who hired him to take their loved ones to the United States.[2] Although he shared profits with an American boss who moved migrants across the border and arranged for safe houses on the US side, Manuel functioned largely as an independent contractor.[3] He chose his customers, set his own rates, determined migration routes, and relied on a flexible network of guides and contacts that he recruited and paid. Manuel had to be strategic in his negotiations with corrupt public officials, hotel staff, bus and taxi drivers, and also with members of criminal organizations on both sides of the US-Mexico border. Like other coyotes, he had to cooperate with criminal groups by paying tolls or moving drugs in order to access parts of the migrant trail controlled by them. Manuel profited from rising violence in crime-ridden areas, the crippling poverty that forced people to incur debts, and the yearning of families to be reunited. However, he was in business to provide a service. His reputation depended on his ability to keep migrants alive and guarantee their arrival in a migration market where chaos and unpredictability reign.[4]

He gave me a choice. He said, "If you marry me I will take care of the smuggling debt. If not, you will have to work to repay the loan I made to you." I said to myself, if this happens it would be too good to be true. The problem was that he was like a friend. I was not attracted to him. It was not at all like this was my man. No, but I thought that I could trust him. So I made the choice and we got married at a church in Matamoros. He explained that he lived in Houston but he would pay someone to take me across the border and would wait for me there.

Isabel's decision to marry her smuggler shows how human smuggling is deeply integrated into the everyday experience of migration. The journey creates a unique social world between departure and arrival where smugglers and migrants are bound together. The reciprocal relationships that develop between them often contradict the accepted constructions of smuggler as predator and migrant as victim. Yet these relationships exist within inherently unequal structures of power exerted by both state authorities and criminal groups.[5]

So the plan was to cross and go through the desert. I walked with a guide for two days through the desert. It was so hard to cross on foot. A number of times I said to the guide, "Just leave me here and I will go back to my country." So we finally made it to a bus terminal and the guide put me on a bus. I slept so soundly and that I forgot where I was. Suddenly I heard a loudspeaker and I woke up and I realized that I was in Houston. When we got to the bus terminal a Spanish-speaking person lent me her cell phone. It was late and Manuel answered right away. He said, "I was so worried. Where are you? Let me talk to the lady in the terminal." I was able to call my mom and found out that she was preparing to return to El Salvador because her visa would expire soon. My heart was broken because after months I had finally made it the US and she was going back home. We had never been separated until she came to the US.

Two days later Manuel and I were reunited. He took me in his arms and said. "Oh my God. You are safe. Your family would have killed me if you had been hurt on the journey." That was a happy time because he treated me really well. He sent money to my father so he could repay the bank loan he took out to finance my trip. So we began to plan a future together. We would settle down, buy a little grocery store, and work together. I convinced him that he should leave his job as a coyote because it was too dangerous. It would be a new life. We had only been together two months when he decided to make one last trip. I didn't want him to go but he said that the money was too good to pass up. We could use it for our business. On his trips north he would always call Señora Chavez when he got to the hotel where I had stayed. Then she would contact me. But the last time he didn't call her. I waited and waited and I was so worried. The next day she had news. He had been drinking in a cantina and a group of rival coyotes had burst in and dragged him away. He disappeared and no one ever found his body. Ten years later, Señora Chavez got in contact to say that the men who kidnapped and killed him, "paid for what they did."

Reports over the last several decades center on the violence suffered by undocumented migrants at the hand of coyotes, cartels, gangs, and corrupt public officials. Less attention has been paid to the restructuring of the business of illicit migration and the mounting competition among smugglers for customers. Since the early 2000s, human smuggling has become a more vertically integrated, centralized criminal enterprise that generates profits rivaling those of drug trafficking and the sex trade. Mexican drug trafficking organizations were ousting long-standing, more informal smuggling operations and beginning to monopolize the routes once controlled by them.[6] Even as secure pathways across Central America and Mexico narrowed, small smuggling entrepreneurs continued to coexist and serve as middlemen with organized criminal operations. Yet Manuel's murder is a stark reminder of the risks involved for small operators, some of whom are as vulnerable as the migrants they guide.[7] Although fifteen years had elapsed since his disappearance, Isabel shed tears at this reminder of how her dream of marriage and stable work evaporated with his death. Border control mechanisms such as checkpoints, inspection sites, detention, and deportation now form a vast containment zone across southern Mexico intended to stem the flow of these migrants.[8]

2006

After that, I had to try to get to my family in Virginia. So I left Texas and a cousin gave me a ride back to Manassas, where I moved in with my oldest brother. I found work in a restaurant. My mom was back to El Salvador and all I did was work to send money for her medical bills. Then, in 2006, on July 15, my father called to say that my mom had been hospitalized and was in a coma. I was so distraught and I was desperate to see her. I came here to work for her and then I decided that I had go back to be with her. When I told my brother, he said, "You are crazy!" I said, "I have to go back because she needs me. She is alone in the hospital." So on July 27 I told my supervisor, "This is my last day." My brother was so furious that he grabbed my bags to stop me from leaving. I said, "Let me go!" So I got on a plane and I went straight to the hospital from the airport. My father was sitting outside and he was shocked to see me. "What did you do? All the things that you went through to get to the US! And now you are here?" I told him, "I had to see her."

One of the nurses took me to her room and whispered to her, "Your daughter is here." It was shocking to see her in that state. She was on oxygen and had tubes inserted everywhere. She was so thin that you could see her bones. She had been unresponsive but when she heard my voice, she opened her eyes. I said, "I am here for you" and I know that she heard me. So I stayed with her until she died on August 28. I was making arrangements for the funeral mass that is planned for the ninth day after the death, when my cousin called me to say that my father had an accident. Later we discovered that he had killed himself rather than live without my mother. That was on the following Saturday, and within one week, I had lost both parents.

After both of my parents died, a friend from the community, Rodrigo, helped me with the funerals. Then everyone left and I felt so alone and depressed. Rodrigo offered to stay and work on the farm. At the beginning he stayed to work but then things changed and we started to live together.

Soon I got pregnant. When I was six months pregnant, he just left one day and never returned. I never understood why. I found myself alone again but this time I was pregnant. So I had the child, a little boy, my Rodrigo.

When the baby was one year old, I met another man who became the father of my second child, a daughter. I was twenty-five years old. He was only eighteen and from the same village. He brought happiness but no experience. He was very willing to work in the fields but the other workers didn't want him there. So he decided to do women's work in the house. He cooked, cleaned, and took care of my baby. He was willing to try anything but he didn't know much. When he changed the diaper, he would put it on backwards and cooking was a real challenge at first. We were together for four years and I was so happy then. When I got home the food was prepared, the house was clean, and my son was bathed. My aunt looked at our situation and teased us saying that he was worse than an old lady in his habits.

He loved the baby and would say that he always wanted a son. I teased him and promised, "When you are old enough I will give you a son." We were like young lovers but because of his age, we hid the relationship from the family. For a woman to be with a younger man was not accepted. Then one of his sisters paid a coyote to take him to the US. He wasn't sure about leaving us but finally he decided to go. He got across the border but was caught in Houston and deported. One day he just showed up back at the farm and I was so happy. In the heat of the moment I forgot to take my [birth control] pill and I got pregnant with Marguerita. I was three months pregnant with her when he made a second attempt to go north. He said that he could support us better from the US. He made it and started to work. Then our baby was born. For a while he stayed in touch and sent money. But then the money and the calls stopped. With distance, things change and love dies.

Isabel spent years back in El Salvador after her parents' death. Then she faced a deadly threat and was forced once again to head north, but this time with two young children in tow.

2013

We fled for our lives when gang members threatened to kill my son and I. People said that the one thing El Salvador had in abundance was gangs. Even in our little canton, gangs were everywhere. I heard that Rodrigo's father had gotten involved with one of the local gangs. He knew that he had a son but had never recognized him. We lost contact after he left me but I would see him in town from time to time. One day, my cousin and I were with my kids outside a local restaurant. Suddenly we heard tires screeching and gun shots. We ran inside the restaurant and hid. I thought that my son was with us but then I realized that he was still outside. His father and Julio, a friend of ours, were together on the other side of the street. The truck stopped and they were struck by a hail of bullets. Several gang members jumped out and threw Julio in back of the truck. Rodrigo's father managed to run away. Poor little Rodrigo saw the whole thing and was screaming, "The gang got my dad. They killed my dad."

The gang dumped Julio's body outside of town. Neighbors finally found Rodrigo's father, who was hiding in a garage. He had lost a lot of blood and we called the police to report the crime. They insisted that they could not leave the station because only one officer was on duty. The truth is that they probably refused to leave the station. Maybe the officer was taking orders from the gang not to investigate. So my cousin took my son's father to the hospital because he was in very bad shape. He left the hospital and went into hiding but we heard that he died of his wounds. People knew that the gang had targeted him and they vowed to kill everyone in his family, especially his son. Gang members started to call me, saying, "We will come for you and your kids unless you pay us." I didn't have any money. Then one night a gang member came out to the farm and grabbed me as I was returning from the fields. He would have raped me if one of the workers had not chased him off. I went to the mayor's office to file a report about what happened. He knew me because he was little Rodrigo's god-father. He wrote a letter explaining that the gang had tried to murder my son's father, had assaulted me at home, and threatened to kill us.

El Salvador has had the highest concentration of gang members per capita in the world for several decades. Gang murders were a major reason that El Salvador had the highest homicide rate in the world—101 homicides per 100,000 people in 2015.[9] Women and children are targeted and murdered by gangs for many reasons, such as if they resist recruitment, report gang crime to the police, refuse to pay extortion demands, are part of families linked to rivals, or if they are gay, lesbian, or bisexual. Gang-related violence is part of a broader pattern of gender and domestic violence against women and children that includes femicide.

I had to leave right away but I couldn't reach Manuel's boss. So a friend lent me money—just $300. In twelve hours, I packed up my kids and left. That trip was not anything like my first one. There were no fancy hotels or guides to lead us. It took us six months to get to the US. We lived from hand to mouth in Mexico because I had nothing and it was so hard to find work. I did odd jobs, we slept outside on plastic bags, we begged and, at times, we were so hungry that we scavenged food from garbage cans. My son lost so much weight and the kids complained about being hungry all the time. Finally, my brother found us in Michoacán and put me in contact with an aunt who had a house on the Mexican side of the border in Matamoros— the same city where I had married Manuel. She sent money so we could go and stay with her there. My son only wanted to know if she could feed us. When we arrived the first thing that he did was to open her refrigerator to see if she really had food! We were starved and exhausted. We stayed with her three months and when it was time to leave, we crossed the border on a bus. I turned myself into Border Patrol. I was not going to try and take two young kids through the desert. We arrived on August 28, 2014.

2014

So, when we were apprehended, I showed the Border Patrol agent the letter from our mayor. He ignored it and screamed at us, "We don't want you here. You're going back." I said, "No, please look at the letter. I want to ask for asylum." A second agent insisted that I had to go back. I pleaded with him to read the letter and he finally did. He said that this letter would give me the right to see an immigration judge. That never happened. First, they put us together in a cell at a Border Patrol station. It was so chaotic, guards were yelling and kids were crying. They put so many families in those freezing cells that we couldn't lie down. The kids were only seven and two at the time and they were terrified. Thank God they didn't separate us. We were held there for three days and then they released us to members of the family in Brownsville, Texas. After three weeks, we came to Virginia and stayed here. I never went to immigration court because I didn't have the money for an attorney. I found out that even with legal status, it could take years for my brother to be able to sponsor me.

Isabel's arrival in 2014 coincided with an unprecedented surge of Central American women and children seeking asylum in the United States. Quickly overwhelmed by the crisis unfolding at the US-Mexico border, the Obama administration reframed the new arrivals as a national security threat and reinstituted a policy of detaining parents with children seeking asylum. The response was chaotic and some families with children, like Isabel's, were released without seeing an immigration judge while others were transferred to immigration detention. Initially, families were detained in a hastily constructed facility in Artesia, New Mexico, that opened on June 27, 2014, and the deportations of asylum seekers began just seventeen days later.[10] Because of egregious due process violations, woefully inadequate medical care, and the systematic mistreatment of parents and children, the Artesia "deportation mill" was closed on December 15, 2014. The government awarded generous no-bid contracts to private companies like the Corrections Corporation of America, renamed to Corps Civic, to open a new, 2,400-bed facility in Dilley, Texas.[11] It began to operate just four days after Artesia closed, on December 19, 2014. The government doubled the size of an existing detention center in Karnes City, Texas.[12] Isabel and her children could have been detained for months in a for-profit immigration prison and subjected to fast track hearings in immigration court. A study of family detention from 2001 to 2016 exposed the extreme barriers migrant families face in gaining legal status. They have been detained in prison settings for long periods and have routinely appeared in immigration court without legal representation. Having an attorney in immigration proceedings is vital to a successful outcome.[13]

2018

So, when we came to Virginia I enrolled Rodrigo in a public elementary school. In the beginning he seemed to be doing well. In fact, both kids were doing okay. I worked a lot and I had help from my brothers' families here. Rodrigo did his homework, was learning English, and played on a soccer team. He helped me a lot with his sister. But that changed this year when he started middle school. There was a crisis in early April. He got into a few fights. A boy on his soccer team kept mocking him and he lost it and jumped on him. He didn't hit him but knocked him down and the principal suspended him for ten days. I didn't understand what he did wrong.

I had to meet with the principal and I told him, "You need to understand that Rodrigo is still adapting to this country. I crossed the border with my two kids in 2014 when he was seven and his sister was just two years old. After what we suffered in El Salvador and Mexico, Rodrigo feels like he has to protect himself and his loved ones. In El Salvador the kids don't have access to a social worker, a counselor, or even the police. If somebody hurts you, you have to respond, you have to take responsibility for yourself." The principal said, "It doesn't work like that here. Your son has serious anger issues and has repeatedly broken the rules by physically attacking other kids. He is a danger to himself and others. You have to have him formally evaluated by a counselor because this was not the first incident. If you don't get an evaluation Rodrigo will not be able to return to school."

Isabel never told the principal about the multiple traumas that Rodrigo experienced from witnessing the gang attack that killed his father and fear that the gang would come for him. There was the sudden and irreparable uprooting from his country, the interrupted schooling, the struggle to survive in Mexico, and the violence of their arrest and detention by immigration authorities. Sustained trauma at a young age can lead to a toxic level of stress and, if prolonged, can affect the brain's structure and function, impairing cognitive and emotional skills. Rodrigo's explosive bouts of anger, loss of control, and recourse to physical violence when bullied suggest that he may have been suffering from post-traumatic stress disorder (PTSD). Any one of these threats to his sense of well-being and security could pose formidable barriers to performing well socially or academically in a US school.[14]

Ligia addressed Isabel, saying:
Rodrigo started a fight on the soccer field and another in the cafeteria. He had to meet with the principal to explain his behavior. He insisted that he had done nothing wrong and that it was the other kids who started it. He raised his voice and demanded to know why they weren't getting into trouble. The principal gave him a warning and a lecture on how to resolve conflicts without violence and to accept responsibility for his actions. Just a week later there was a really disturbing incident. Two girls called him a name and when they walked away, he grabbed one by the hair and dragged her backward. When she tried to pull away he tightened his grip and yanked her arm. He didn't let go until she screamed. That time a number of students and a hall monitor saw what happened. When there is a fight it can be hard to know who is at fault. But in this case, it was very, very clear that your son started it.

Growing defensive, Isabel insisted:
The only place my son has problems is in school. At home he is fine. He comes right home everyday and spends twenty-five minutes on his homework. Then he cleans up his room and the kitchen and watches his little sister for me. Things are fine. I still don't know why he was suspended.

Ligia responded:
Look, he has a problem with authority. He challenged the principal and he keeps getting into fights. We need to find out what triggers the aggressive behavior. The principal wants an evaluation and to develop an individual plan for him. It is called a 504. We have to know if he needs treatment. If that is the case, the school will work with you. Believe me, we don't want this behavior recorded as defiance or labeled as Oppositional Defiant Disorder.

The 504 referral is designed to determine whether a student qualifies as disabled and needs special educational services. Teachers and counselors make recommendations based on their assessments of the student's behavior, the social and cultural background, and evidence of physical or psychological impairment. Conditions such as Attention Deficit Hyperactivity Disorder (ADHD) and Oppositional Defiant Disorder (ODD) qualify as disabilities. Ligia knew that the school administration viewed a diagnosis of ODD as problematic. The Diagnostic and Statistical Manual of Mental Disorders, 5th Edition, defines ODD as a constellation of behaviors including defiance toward authority, refusal to follow rules, and explosive outbursts of anger. Psychologists view treatment as critical because ODD is often accompanied by "other serious mental disorders." If left untreated, it can develop into "conduct disorder," a more disruptive condition that puts young people at risk for delinquent activity and substance abuse.[15]

Isabel continued:
No, you forget that Rodrigo was doing really well on the soccer team and then because of that problem with one of his teammates, he quit the team. So I made an appointment with a counselor at the Community Services Board. I am not justifying his behavior. I know that he broke the rules but the others really push his buttons. I told him, "Don't pay attention to them. They are the real losers."

When Rodrigo found out that he had to see a counselor he got mad and, at first, he refused to go. 'Go see a shrink?? No way! I am not crazy.' But I told him that it is different here. People don't think the same way about it. Counselors are there to help you. So he saw the counselor and liked her. She told him, "You can't solve anything with physical force and you can't control others. You can only control yourself." She warned him that if he couldn't do that he could end up in jail. She asked Rodrigo why he gets so angry. He admitted that he is very unhappy in school. He says that the other kids don't like him and make fun of him. He is very depressed and anxious. When I talk to him about school, he gets so upset and sad. He says, "They laugh at me—everything about me: my clothes, my accent, the way I look. The Black kids are the worst to deal with. They are the racists. Some days I feel like I just want to die." He has said so many times how happy he was back home. He loved the farm and wants to go back, to be with his friends and family, and just harvest corn. He seems lost. He has no friends and has started wandering around outside alone. I call him on his phone and he doesn't answer. The house and the farm are still there and one of my cousins is living there and managing things. My older brother who has legal status here goes back and forth to check on things. He says everything is fine. I wonder what would be the best thing to do? Should I insist that he stay here? Allow him to return to El Salvador? Would he be safe from the gangs if he goes back?"

The remittances sent home from migrants in the United States allow poor families to buy land and to build a modest patrimony. Yet this patrimony rests on a shaky foundation, threatened by the constant need for labor in a subsistence economy and the lack of basic public services such as health care, running water, and electricity. Medical bills for cancer spell economic ruin and, in this case, prompted a desperate compromise. Isabel married a smuggler she barely knew. In contrast to her father and brothers who had legal status and could travel freely, Isabel was forced to cross the border illegally and on foot through unforgiving desert terrain. It was a gamble that could have ended very differently.

This story belies the all too common experience of domestic violence and family breakdown in Central America and Mexico. It is a testament to the power of family and, especially, the bonds between mothers and daughters in the face of relentless adversity. Isabel was also deeply devoted to her father. She recalled the trauma of burying him so soon after her mother's passing. "It was the worst day of my life. I was frozen in place. I couldn't swallow." In addition to losing her parents, Isabel lived in several informal unions and had children by two different men. Her experience with multiple intimate partners confirms a regional pattern where it is rare for fathers to be a consistent presence in family life whether they migrate or not. Gendered ideologies maintain and justify paternal distance because they view men as largely unable to stay with one intimate partner or to remain connected to their children.[16]

Susie Stratham, a Mexican-born counselor in the Fairfax public schools, described her work with immigrant kids from poor families:

> There is so much discrimination in this country against kids with darker skin. Americans lump all Hispanics in the same group. They say these illegals are uneducated and don't know any better. I know better because I came here as a migrant with a young daughter. These kids come from places where the concept of mental health doesn't exist. They think that you are crazy if you go to a psychologist. I myself was not aware of the psychological impact of separation and migration on these kids until I saw their issues in school: disrespect for authority, truancy, drug and gang involvement. Most of them feel like they don't belong in school. They don't understand why it is important. They just want to work.[17]

The need to accept individual responsibility and be accountable for one's actions is a lecture that most American teenagers will hear repeatedly, particularly if they act out. Given the violence that Rodrigo experienced growing up, that lecture rang hollow. In a Salvadoran hamlet where gangs acted with impunity and often infiltrated the police, self-defense was a matter of life and death. In his rural community, nearly everyone was related and dependent on one another for support and survival. There was no social welfare net to soften the harshness of local life. Working the land was the norm and schooling an afterthought.

How could Rodrigo realistically succeed in a suburban Virginia school where literacy in English and formal credentials were paramount? How could he adjust to a school where the ethnic and racial divisions among his school peers were a complete mystery to him? It is no wonder that he longed to exchange one hostile land for another one where, despite the danger from gangs, at least he was known and loved.

5

María's Story

"I Don't Care if They Are Listening. Come Back Here."

María agrees to meet at a McDonald's in Northern Virginia. Because her husband is in hiding after being deported a second time, she refuses to discuss where they live. She arrives with her youngest child—a rambunctious four-year-old girl who gobbles up the Happy Meal I purchase for her and makes friends with an older couple who are sitting close by.

2000

The coyote took us to El Naranjo, Guatemala, close to the border with Mexico. A few days after turning eighteen, I had left El Salvador with my eighteen-month-old baby girl and her godfather, Benite. I had no reason to stay in El Salvador. My husband had left me for another woman and I was completely alone, living with my child in a big house that I had inherited from my grandparents. I had no siblings, my mother was dead, and my father was living in the US. Trouble started as soon as my husband left, because people knew that I had no man to protect me. They began stealing things outside the house and then they started on the roof. At night I could hear them walking up there and removing the shingles. When that happened, my heart would race and I could barely breathe. One night I woke up and heard men with hammers and crowbars making a hole in the roof. They got into a storage area attached to the house and reached the inside door. Thank God that I had locked it but they started trying to break it down. I screamed so loudly that the neighbors came and chased the men away. After that, I went to Don Antonio's house, a respected man in the town, and I asked for his help. He was a friend of my daughter's grandparents and I thought he could appeal to them to help us. The problem was that they didn't believe that their son was the baby's father. So they refused.

I went to a neighbor who had the only telephone in the village and called my father in LA. I said, "I want to come to the US. I have no future here." He said that it was a bad idea for me to travel alone with a baby. His brother was also in the US and he was the one who convinced my father to let me come. They agreed to share the coyote's fees and they arranged the trip. I had had no contact with my husband for months and so I went to the consulate by myself to get a travel document for my daughter. I had to show them her birth certificate and that created a problem because my husband was listed as the father. They told me I needed his permission to take her out of the country. I lied and said he was dead. Then, of course, they required proof of his death. I started to panic because I was scheduled to leave in a few days.

Although I hated to face my husband, I went to his house and asked him to sign the required forms. He got furious and ripped them up. So I went back to Don Antonio in tears and explained that I had the money to leave but my husband wouldn't sign the papers. At first Don Antonio tried to convince me to leave the baby with him because he only had a son. I was shocked and said, "No! My daughter is not a dog to leave behind. She goes with me." His wife understood and pleaded with him to help me. So Don Antonio arranged a meeting with José, a coyote he knew who lived close by. When José heard that there were two "clients"—an eighteen-year-old girl with a baby and an angry husband—he raised the fee to $15,000. So Don Antonio devised a plan for his son Benite to come with me and to pose as the baby's father. Benite and I were school friends and about the same age. José agreed and at Don Antonio's urging reduced his fee by several thousand dollars. It was still much higher than if I had left alone. We had to leave very quickly because we were all afraid that my husband would try to stop us. We left very early the next morning.

It was common knowledge that María's husband had left her and that she lived alone with a toddler. Salvadoran women who head their own households and live without male protection are particularly vulnerable. There is a numbing regularity to the tales they tell of lawlessness and male predation. As we have seen, they cannot count on protection from the police or courts but are subject to paternalistic rules on child custody and travel outside the country. The father's paternity allowed him to prevent the child's departure from El Salvador despite his refusal to support María and his baby. It is no small irony that María's migration relied almost exclusively on a network of men—a prominent local, her father, her uncle, a childhood friend, and a network of smugglers.

The plan was for us to cross into Mexico on buses, head north along the coast, and finally end up in Matamoros on the Texas border. To get through the checkpoint at El Naranjo, we were told to slip a hundred pesos into the passport when the customs official checked it. The night before we left Guatemala, I decided to risk going out of the hotel where we were staying. No one would think that a single mother would try to cross the border with an eighteen-month-old baby. Benite and I went to a store to buy pampers and to call my dad. We were holding hands and passed a Guatemalan policeman who never bothered us.

At 5:00 in the morning, we got on the bus and headed for the checkpoint. The coyote sat in the seat in front of us and Benite and I were behind with the baby between us. We looked like a young happy family going on a trip. Only minutes later, Mexican soldiers stopped the bus and started to check everyone's papers. I began to tremble but the coyote signaled for us to stay calm. Because he had a Mexican visa they didn't bother him. But one of the soldiers asked for our passports. Benite handed them over and said, "She is my wife and this is our little girl and we are going to Matamoros." The soldier checked our passports, looked at us closely, and then signaled to Benite and the coyote to follow him. As they went up the isle the soldier gestured for a few other riders to get out of the bus. I was terrified because Benite had all our money and I had nothing—no passports, no IDs, no maps. A half hour dragged by and one of the soldiers tapped on the window and gave the driver the sign to leave. At that moment I remembered my father warning me that my baby could die on this trip. I had snapped back at him, "Well then we will die together." I wondered then if he was right.

I ran to the front of the bus and told the driver that they had taken my husband and that I had no money or papers. He asked me quietly where I was from and I didn't lie. I told him that we were from El Salvador and headed north. He nodded and said that he understood how hard the journey but he had the other passengers to consider. He hesitated and then said that he could wait for five minutes. If my husband didn't return I would have to get off and wait there. I was frantic standing at the window and praying that they would come back. The driver started the engine and began to close the door. Just then I saw Benite and José shouting and running toward the bus. The driver stopped and let them on. I burst into tears. The soldiers had returned our papers but they had to pay a bribe of a thousand pesos, not a hundred, as we thought.

So we made it all the way to Matamoros, across from Brownsville on the US side. We went to a house that was rented by coyotes for migrants waiting to cross the border. José and Benite had to return to El Salvador. We were so grateful to them because they took a big risk by bringing me with the baby. José said that he was happy he helped us but it was so hard for me to say goodbye to Benite.

A Honduran woman and her Mexican husband were the caretakers of the house. Soon after, an American named Anna arrived. She spoke Spanish really well and handled the smuggling of migrants across the Rio Bravo. Anna gave me three impossible choices: to cross the river with the baby in my arms, to hide in the back of a big trailer truck or to have her pose as the baby's grandmother and cross "legally." I called my dad and he said that we had to trust Anna. So for the privilege of using my daughter's birth certificate, my father had to pay Anna an extra $1,000. We had given José half of the money when we left, a quarter when we crossed into Mexico, and the final quarter had to be sent to Anna before we crossed the border. She was saying things like "Do you know how lucky you were to make it to the US border? Most people get deported from El Naranjo." She warned me, "You will never make it to Virginia with the baby. Why not just stay here with me?" Then, finally my dad wired the money and the crossing was set for that night.

The hardest thing I ever did was to let Anna take my baby. She left and told us to wait for the guides who would take us across the river that night. We were supposed to leave at 10:00 but no one came for hours. I was sick with worry and so afraid. Would I make it? Would I see my baby again? They finally came at 4:20 a.m. and my heart sank. I thought, my God, could these guys be the coyotes? They were skinny and had tattoos all over. They were not wearing shirts and it seemed like they were high on drugs. There were seven in our group and one of the other migrants whispered to me, "Look at those guys. They are the lowest of the low. They take on the most dangerous jobs, make the least amount of money, and risk their lives the most. They do it to get drug money and are always high." There was no time for hesitation. The coyotes told us, "Come on, let's go."

We made it across the river and climbed over a barbed wire fence and ran through dense brush before we met Anna's people at 7:30 in the morning. It was September 25, 2000. They took us to a house near the border in Texas where we were able to call our families. Later in the morning two guides, not Anna, brought my baby to that house. She was barefoot and only wearing a tee shirt. She was dirty and she was hungry. I asked where her clothes were and they claimed that she had just woken up and wasn't dressed yet. I didn't dare challenge them because I was just relieved to have her back and to be in the US. From there, we went to Anna's house and we were able to wash and change our clothes. Then they put us on a Greyhound bus to Houston.

We came to a checkpoint and the problems started. Immigration officials boarded the bus and they asked for my papers. I had none and I had to turn myself in. So they took me off the bus and they questioned me but allowed me to call my dad. He reminded me about his sister Carmen who lived in Houston. The officer talked with my dad and took down Carmen's name, address, and phone number. The same officer called my Aunt Carmen and told her that I would get to Houston in three to four hours.

I couldn't believe it! He gave me food and water for the baby and handed me fifty dollars to pay for the bus trip. He told the driver to take me to a particular station and to make sure the woman who met me was my aunt. I couldn't believe it after what had happened to us in Mexico. It was a long ride but I had money and the driver spoke Spanish. When we left, he said, "Good luck and God bless you."

María was the only mother I interviewed who smuggled a baby across the US-Mexico border despite dire warnings that the plan was reckless and likely to end in tragedy. All along the way, she encountered an industry that turns migrants into commodities and sets their value in a parallel economy controlled by corrupt public officials, smugglers, gangs, and cartels. Migrants gain value as labor to exploit, bodies to prostitute, and lives to exchange for cash. A young mother migrating with a baby represented a high risk and a high exchange value because they were difficult "cargo" to smuggle. But migrants can also lose value along the way. María's exchange value was only guaranteed if she and her baby made it across the border alive. Had she and the baby been apprehended, deported, kidnapped, or killed, their exchange value would have plummeted, representing a loss to the family, Don Antonio, and, especially, the smugglers.[1]

In 2000, the route through Naranjo was new and the border was relatively porous. A small bribe got them into Mexico. In contrast, at the Texas border, María encountered tighter border security and a more organized smuggling operation. Gone was the personalized connection she had enjoyed with Don Antonio's smuggler José. To navigate the US border, José contracted with a South Texas criminal operation that employed a web of recruiters, drivers, lookouts, and guides to do the dangerous work of moving migrants across the Rio Grande and avoiding Customs and Border Protection agents. Coordinating the operation was an American manager who found safe houses, arranged pickups, and collected the cash. As a white US citizen, she was able to pose as the baby's grandmother and cross "legally" at a US port of entry. Her decision to personally assume the risk of smuggling a baby into the US demanded a large surcharge.[2] María had extraordinarily good luck when she met a Texas Border Patrol agent who gave her money and ensured her safe release to her aunt. Had she arrived in 2018 under the Trump administration's zero-tolerance policy, she could have been separated from her baby, jailed, prosecuted for illegal entry, and deported.

I lived with Aunt Carmen and her family for a month. They were so good to me and the whole family loved my baby so much. She had great plans for me and promised to support me so I could go back to school. I was beginning to make plans for myself and to feel safe again. But then my husband found out that I had made it to the U.S. and he began calling me. He said he had separated from the other woman and insisted that he wanted to get back together. He asked me to forgive him for abandoning us and was trying to convince me to go live with his sister in Virginia. Meanwhile, his sister connected me with a relative of his who lived in Houston. She called and insisted that I leave Carmen's house and go to stay with her family. I thought about what to do and although I loved Carmen and was so thankful for her help, I finally gave in. To this day I am not sure why I did that. How do I explain it? I didn't really know my dad's family. He left when I was really young. But this was my husband and this was his child and I had to give him another chance. I wrote a letter to my Aunt Carmen and left it in her bedroom the same day I left. When Carmen came home from work we were gone and she was so upset. The whole family couldn't believe that I left of my own free will and they searched for me all that day and the next. They were furious that I left after Aunt Carmen had been so good to me. They said that I was turning my back on my family and an education and for what? To return to the man who had abandoned me? Who had mistreated me? They reminded me that he ignored me until I left him and made it to the US. My father's whole family refused to speak to me for almost four years after I did that.

The wife of my husband's cousin came to Aunt Carmen's house to pick me up. She put us on a bus to Virginia from Houston but she didn't give me enough money for the trip. Things went from bad to worse when I got to Woodbridge. We had to go to stay with my husband's brother who had an extra room. And they insisted that I pay rent. I obviously didn't have any money at that point so they made us sleep in the attic. It was horrible, dirty, cold and there were only storage boxes and an old mattress on the floor. Plus, they had a four-year boy who was so rough. He would hit my daughter, pull her hair, push her down, and once, he shoved her head into the toilet. They never punished him and that really hurt me. I was stuck, I had no job, and I didn't know anyone.

A few weeks later I met a Salvadoran lady in the park and she listened to my story and eventually we became like sisters. She helped me to find work and her mother agreed to watch my daughter. When I told my husband's brother that I was looking for another place to live, they said I owed them $400 in rent for that attic! I paid it but on the condition that they give my daughter and I our own bedroom. They did and I began to work three jobs. One in the early morning from Monday to Saturday, another in the afternoon during the week and on Saturday night, and I worked in a restaurant on Sundays. My goal was to save enough money to bring my husband to the US. I kept the cell number of José, the coyote, and in less than a year I had saved $3,000. I asked José to bring my husband. He scolded me: "Oh the things that you have done for that man!" He charged me the amount that I had saved and said that I could pay him the rest later. So following the same route, my husband arrived at the house in Matamoros. The caretakers said to him: "Oh you are the one you deserted your wife and child. We know all about you!" When he finally arrived in the US he was chastened and he never misbehaved again.

Things looked so hopeful when my husband made it to the same house in Brownsville where I was reunited with my daughter the year before. Hours later immigration officials raided the house and took everyone to jail. After ten days, he was released on bond with a notice to appear in immigration court in Harlingen. Instead of going to court, he headed straight to Virginia to begin a life with us.

2007

My husband learned how to install carpets and he started his own business in 2006. By that time, we had two kids, the daughter who came with me and a son who was born here in 2002. It was going so well that he bought tools and a used van. We had two healthy kids and a good life. We rented a nice apartment, had a regular income and we could even eat out sometimes. But then, in January 2007, the police stopped my husband because he had a broken taillight. When he didn't have a license they did a background check and saw that he had an outstanding deportation order from Texas. He called to tell me that he was being deported. The police followed him home and he had only five minutes before they took him to jail. His big worry was that I would be left alone with two kids and only one salary to pay the rent on the apartment. He gave me all the cash he had in his wallet and told me to sell the van and his tools so I could pay the bills. My daughter was nine by then and she understood what was happening. She ran to the police officers and begged them to let him go. But it was too late and they took him.

The next day a bail bondsman in Fairfax told us that my husband did not have the right to bail and that he would be turned over to ICE in twenty-four hours. I found an attorney who charged us $3,500 to take his case. So I sold the van and gave him all the money. I was desperate. Then I got word that my husband was in an ICE detention center in Richmond and gave that information to the attorney. I asked him if that attorney had ever come to the detention facility to see him. No, he just took the money and never did anything. My husband called me before they deported him to El Salvador. That was February 9. I was torn up inside and I said to him: "I don't care if they are listening. You come back here as soon as you can." That same spring, he got across the border without any problems. We used the same coyote and by this time, José was like family.

2018

I brought my youngest with me today. She was born in 2013 and is four years old. As you can see she is very active. When I came to the US eighteen years ago, it was such a different time. In 2001 all Salvadorans got Temporary Protected Status (TPS) because of the destruction caused by big earthquakes in our country. My father had been in the US for years. He got legal status and then became a US citizen, so I can get permanent status through him.

But my husband is a different story. Since he came across the last time, he lives in the shadows and is not the same man. He can't drive, he can't start a business, and now if he finds work, someone else is the boss. We had to leave the apartment we rented because people knew that my husband came back across the border after being deported. In fact, we have moved twice since and now live with family in Maryland. My son was in high school in Virginia but had to change schools. He is confused and angry because of his father's situation and he has acted out in school. We live from one day to the next.

Navigating life in 2018 was, as María said, very different from in 2000. In January 2001, just three months after she arrived in the United States, a series of earthquakes, the largest measuring 7.7 on the Richter scale, hit El Salvador. The quakes leveled homes, displaced one million people and created a humanitarian crisis. The Bush administration granted Temporary Protected Status (TPS) to Salvadorans already living in the United States when the quakes struck. With TPS, Salvadorans got temporary legal status that shielded them from deportation and allowed them to work legally. María was eligible for TPS, but her husband, who arrived just a month later, was not.

In January 2018, three months before our interview, Department of Homeland Security (DHS) secretary Kirstjen Nielsen announced the termination of TPS for El Salvador, claiming that the original crisis no longer existed. It made no difference that El Salvador had the highest

homicide rate in the world outside a war zone and a huge gang population. In 2021, the Biden administration issued new TPS designations for
the countries experiencing armed conflict, environmental disasters, or
disease epidemics, including El Salvador. If this had not happened, the
402,000 TPS holders—half of whom are Salvadoran—could have been
forcibly removed from the United States.[3] Because TPS holders are the
parents of some 273,000 US citizens, most under twenty-one years of
age, like María's two youngest children, it could have turned "into the
largest family-separation operation in American history."[4]

The larger questions María asked herself were: Why did she exchange a lov-
ing home with her father's relatives and the chance to get an education
for an uncertain future with the man who had deserted her in El Salvador?
Why did she travel across country and stay with his family when they mistreated her? Why work three jobs to pay a smuggler to bring him to the
United States? Perhaps the answer lies in the losses she had endured and
the limited choices she had. María had no grandmother or mother and no
real relationship with her father or his relatives. Forgiving the man she loved
and supporting his migration may have been a calculated wager to gain
security and rebuild a family headed by the father of her children. María
had few skills, little formal education, spoke no English, and migrated under
duress. She may have seen the promise of opportunity in the United States
as an illusion. The decision to cede control over her life to her husband's
family may have been a necessary compromise between what she could
imagine in a new land and what she could realistically expect. For a time,
the successes of María and her husband exceeded all expectations. They
built a thriving business, had two more children, and lived well. Sadly, the
disintegration of their life following her husband's deportation was not a
failure of imagination but the result of a broken immigration system.

6

Nohely's Story

"In Mexico the Zetas Tried to Extort Money from Us"

It is a beautiful day in April 2018 when we meet with Nohely's son Javier. He lives with his mother, stepfather, and four half siblings in a modest ranch house in a quiet subdivision in Northern Virginia. At sixteen, Javier is the oldest of five children; his siblings range in age from thirteen to four years old. We meet all the kids and the family dog, a sweet little mutt who yaps and jumps in excitement when we arrive. Javier's mother, Nohely, asks one of the kids to lock the dog in a bedroom. She tells us that she and Javier were separated for most of his life. Nohely left Honduras to work in the United States when Javier was just two years old. His father stayed in the country where he worked as a policeman in an anti-drug-trafficking unit. After one successful drug bust, the traffickers retaliated by ambushing and brutally murdering four members of the unit, including his father. At that point, Javier went to live with his mother's parents in the Honduran city of Tocoa in the department of Colón. He recalled a happy childhood until one day in 2016 when his life was turned upside down.

2016

Javier:

With the money my mom sent, I was able to go to a good private school. It was different from the local public schools. There were no drugs or dealing, only a few cliques, and no real conflicts. Occasionally there would be fights but mostly it was a good school. I learned a lot there. After school, I was always outside with my friends. Every day we would go to the local mall and then play sports. We knew all our neighbors and we would talk to them. I lived there for fourteen years and never had a problem until one day. My grandmother had said that my cousin and I could go out. We were on the way to play soccer and all of a sudden members of a local gang attacked us. My cousin was the target and he escaped but the gang members beat me real bad and left me lying unconscious in the street. They didn't even take my cell phone so we understood that it was a warning.

His mother, Nohely, spoke up:
After that happened, I had to get him out of there. He was not yet fifteen years old.

Javier:
I was so afraid. For two weeks after that happened I was too scared to go outside. I was bruised all over and when I did go out I completely changed my daily routine. My grandparents insisted that I go to the hospital and they took x-rays of my skull because they had kicked me in the head several times. I was not seriously hurt. At that point we decided that it was time for me to leave.

Nohely:
So my son made three attempts to get to the US. We used a coyote that the family recommended. The first time, he was caught at the border with Mexico and he was immediately deported back to Honduras. He was only held in a reception center for a few days and then my father picked him up. Three weeks later he made a second attempt with a group, and when he was going through Mexico, the trouble started. The first call I got was from a guy who claimed that he was a policeman. He said, "We have your son and his friends. They are in the jail at the police station." He asked me for money. I said, "We can't send any money." So they hung up and the next day I got another call and they threatened to hurt Javier if I didn't send them money. Thank God that my son didn't know about the threats. He spent a week in that jail cell at the police station with three older men. He was not mistreated but the place was filthy and the food was bad.

The migration of Central American unaccompanied children fleeing their homes in the Northern Triangle countries of El Salvador, Guatemala, and Honduras reached crisis levels in the summer of 2014. The United States outsourced the interdiction and removal of Central American migrants by funding Mexico's Southern Border Plan. The plan imposed draconian immigration enforcement measures that were designed to stop migrants at the border with Guatemala and to apprehend them along popular transit routes to the United States. With funding from the United States, Mexico intensified roadside checkpoints, raids, apprehensions, detentions, and deportations. Between 2014 and 2016, Mexico had one of the highest detention rates in the world.[1] In 2015, Mexican authorities apprehended more than 20,000 unaccompanied minors from Northern Triangle countries and deported over 14,000 of them. In 2016, the year Javier migrated, Mexico apprehended fewer minors (17,500) but deported more than the preceding year (15,000).[2] Despite formal legal protections for unaccompanied minors, the reality on the ground was quite different. After their apprehension, Central American minors were often placed in jails or detention centers with unrelated adults where there was inadequate food, little space for recreation, and no educational services. Few were screened to determine their eligibility for asylum or given information about other forms of protection. In fact, less than 1 percent of the 17,500 unaccompanied children apprehended in 2016 in Mexico filed an asylum claim.[3] Instead, the majority were eventually deported to the dangerous situations they fled.

Nohely:
From there, they sent him to a DIF [Sistema para el Desarrollo Integral de la Familia] shelter for minors in Mexico. At that point someone different called and tried to extort money from us. He demanded that we send them money or they would cut him to pieces and send me a picture. The caller said, "If you don't send the money now you will spend it for his funeral later." We think that it was someone on the shelter staff who was also on the payroll of the Zetas. He had our address and phone numbers. We think

that he got it from the shelter files. What they do is to keep calling to see who gets caught in the trap. They want to send the kids back so they extort the parents. If you send the money and then try to call the number they give you, it doesn't work. When they called I told them that I didn't have any more money and I explained that I had borrowed the money for Javier's trip from my brother. They said, "Give me his number." I said, "Wait, I will call you back." It was always the same story. They either never picked up or the number didn't work. Then I began to get texts from a different person who was also trying to extort money from me. They sent several messages saying, "We need the money or we will deport your son. We know where his grandparents live. We will burn down their house and then send the Maras to kill them."

Javier spent almost a month in the DIF shelter before they deported him to a shelter in Guatemala and then sent him back to Honduras. I didn't know what to do. I felt a lot of pressure. They would send messages from one number and tell you to call them back on another cell. Even after he was deported back to Honduras the second time I was still receiving text messages that said: "He finally made it to the US and we need you to call us back at this number. It is urgent! Your son needs money." So Javier waited about ten days in Honduras before he tried a third time and that time he made it. It took about ten days but he finally got across the border.

Mexican law requires that immigration authorities transfer migrant children, who are initially housed in jails or detention centers, to state-run shelters with services tailored to their needs known as the Mexican System for Integral Family Development or DIF. The DIF facilities are required by law to provide adequate food, education, health care, appropriate shelter, legal counsel, and consular representation to all children housed in their facilities. Even after significant efforts to increase capacity at DIF shelters, they lacked both the space and the resources to accommodate the increased number of Central American minors who were detained beginning in 2014.[4] Even those who were fortunate enough to be transferred to DIF facilities still viewed them as detention.

Minors stayed at the facilities 24/7. They did not attend local schools and had no supervised visits to local parks or playgrounds.

The Los Zetas criminal syndicate is believed to be Mexico's largest drug cartel. Founded by thirty-one ex-members of the Mexican army and Guatemalan Special Forces in the late 1990s, its operations now extend along the country's northern and southern borders, throughout Central America, and in various cities in the United States. Members of the Los Zetas cartel infiltrate many sectors of Mexican society in the areas they control; they maintain control through the payment of bribes to office holders and public officials in the military, police, prisons, and courts. Over the last two decades, the Zetas have diversified their illicit activities to include the lucrative business of kidnapping and extorting undocumented migrants and their families. When families are contacted by criminal organizations demanding money, rather than alert the authorities, they typically try to negotiate payment directly with the gang or cartel members.[5] Javier continued his story:

I didn't really mind being in that shelter in Mexico even though we couldn't leave. I got along with all the kids. I played around, joked, and had fun. We didn't have school and there wasn't much to do so I slept a lot. I was the youngest one at fourteen and the others would tease me and we would arm wrestle. Nobody believed that I was fourteen years old because I was so tall compared to the other kids. They respected me because they didn't believe that I was a minor.

In my first two attempts to leave home, the coyote was caught. He told us before we left home that if the Mexican military police caught us we were supposed to say that we didn't know him. There is a severe penalty for human trafficking so the coyote said if he got caught I was on my own. So that happened twice. The third time I traveled with a woman and her little daughter. The coyote for the last trip was a friend of my grandfather's and he was really good. He charged the equivalent of $5,500 for the whole trip. It included everything, food, transportation, all the bribes he would need to pay and it covered three attempts. He was an Evangelical Protestant. He never said bad words. He stressed good living and the importance of being moral. Despite his strong Christian beliefs, he never tried to convert me. He did give me advice throughout the journey. He told me that it is important to keep good company and never to do drugs. He had lived in the US and arranged for us to stay in hotels on the trip north.

At first, I was really afraid because of the stories of kidnapping and murder. Once we left, the journey was a challenge but also kind of cool. Like extreme sports when you have to run fast and hide in the dark at times. I got to see all kinds of nature, different trees, and animals. It was amazing. I remember once that we had to walk a long way and it was pouring rain and the ground got muddy and slippery and the people with us started to fall and slide down. It was really tough going.

When we were in Guatemala we got stopped by the military police and the coyote paid them off. We were in a mini bus and they stopped us and they wanted him to get off. The coyote negotiated so he could stay on the bus. At that point he thought about leaving me behind because my height attracted too much attention. In Guatemala, the people are really short. When we went to go from Guatemala into Mexico we had to cross a river in a boat and we saw alligators in that river! When we went through Mexico, at one point we spent two hours hiding until someone came to pick us up.

The woman with the child needed help with her bags. The coyote and I helped them when we had long distances to walk. We came to a place where a car picked us up. It was a really fast car. The ride was fast and wild. That last trip we only rode in cars or vans because it is safer that way. The first time I took public buses in Mexico. That was a mistake because with a bus you always run the risk that it will be stopped and la migra will check papers. There are also military police. If they question you and you pretend you don't understand or don't cooperate they start hitting you right away. They don't fool around. The coyote told us if the military police stopped us and told us to get off the bus, we should obey immediately. He explained that they have uniforms that are black and blue. I had a cell phone and the whole time I stayed in touch with my mom and my grandparents. My mom was really anxious but I was excited. I couldn't believe that this was happening.

So, things changed when we got close to the US border. There are smugglers who specialize in crossing the [Rio Grande] river. They control river crossings and charge $1,000 just to get across. The coyote has to pay them and they don't allow anyone else on their turf. I don't know if they were in a gang but they had lots of tattoos and made their living as gate-keepers of the border. They took us to a house and made us leave behind our cell phones so they could make sure that there was no way to track us. I saw an exchange of money between our coyote and with the man of the house. They brought inflatables and told us to get into them in order to cross the river. It was night and very dark and the water did not look deep. We crossed to the other side and then they left us and went back to Mexico.

They didn't tell us where to go. They didn't give us any instructions. I was still with the woman and her daughter so we started to walk. We were on a dirt road and came to the crossroad and we didn't know whether we should turn right or left. We had no idea. So, I said, "Let's go right." I became the guide at that point.

Nohely cut in:
Yes, but they didn't pay you!

Javier:
I had to keep deciding which way to go as we went on. I found out later that we were in Texas. We walked for about a half hour, there was a lot of brush and abandoned shacks. We saw signs that said, 'Trespassers will be shot.' We saw surveillance cameras and a lot of barbed wire. Then we saw a sign that said, 'Welcome to Texas.' I screamed, 'Hey we are in Texas.' We were so happy and then we came to a big bridge and soon after US immigration found us. They held us in that area and took our information. They told us that a bus was coming. At first they joked with us and said, 'It will be cool inside that bus. I bet that you don't have air conditioned buses in your country.' They gave us a ham sandwich on bread. It was horrible . . . it was nearly frozen. Then the bus arrived and it was a fast trip to the border patrol station.

Things really changed once we got there. The guards told us to get undressed. They were really rude and yelled, 'Hurry up.' They swore at us and one guy called me a son of a bitch. It was so humiliating. They treated a man who was with us even worse. They screamed at him and shoved him against the wall. We spent one day at that station in the cold cell. It actually wasn't that cold but I couldn't sleep because of the noise and the cell was so crowded that we couldn't lie down. We heard other people arguing and insults were flying. There was a big Black guard who got so mad and came over and said to them, 'Shut up you sons of bitches.' We spent one night there and I called my aunt and uncle because my grandparents didn't have a phone. My uncle didn't answer because he has a disco and there was so much noise that he couldn't hear the phone. So I called back at midnight. It was New Year's Eve.

Since its creation nearly one hundred years ago, the Border Patrol has been steeped in a culture of institutional racism. The routine abuse of migrants with near impunity is a by-product of a Border Patrol culture that dehumanizes and demeans border crossers.[6] Former Border Patrol agent, Jenn Budd, has said, "In the academy they mandate and teach agents to use racist terms for migrants so they see these people as 'others' that are not like them . . . if you aren't willing to be harsh toward the migrants that you encounter then you are judged by that and that reflects on whether or not they retain you."[7] In 2012, a Customs and Border Protection (CBP) use-of-force instructor reported to ICE's Office of Professional Responsibility that one of his colleagues had told a room of supervisors, "You tell all the guys that if they feel threatened, they can beat that tonk like a piñata until the candy comes out." In federal court, a Border Patrol agent testified that "tonk" is the sound when a "wetback" is hit over the head with a flashlight.[8] The Border Patrol may perpetrate violence through less direct means, including medical abuse and neglect, inhumane custody conditions, and, more recently, the punitive separation of parents and children.[9] Over time, CBP has become a sprawling, well-funded and immensely powerful law enforcement agency. Despite numerous lawsuits, the CBP continues to receive generous funding from Congress and enjoys an extraordinary degree of independence.

The reports of Border Patrol agents saying racial slurs, sexual comments, and other offensive language were not limited to use against adult migrants. When the number of unaccompanied minors in federal custody in the United States nearly doubled in 2012, attorneys with the Women's Refugee Commission interviewed 151 children. Many children reported that they had been treated harshly while in CBP custody. Texas Border Patrol agents had shoved and kicked them, tasered them even when they were compliant, and destroyed or threw away their only possessions, including family bibles. One agent held a gun to a youth's head to dissuade him from escaping and another kicked over the cot of a sleeping boy, dumping him onto the floor.[10] Two years later, as unaccompanied children flooded CBP stations, reports of the systematic abuse of these children by Border Patrol agents again made headlines. The mistreatment included body cavity searches, shackling, denial of food and medical services, as well as verbal, physical, and sexual abuse.[11]

Javier:
After that night they transferred us to the kennel cages. I spent two and one-half days there. The food was better. They gave us sandwiches that tasted better and chips. Sometimes they gave us five sandwiches each. There was a lotta food. But there were twenty-five of us in one of those cages. I wasn't sleeping so they pulled me out and made me sit in a corner of the cell by myself. They told me that I had to sleep. The guard that day was really nasty. In the afternoon of the third day, they took me to the airport and I flew to Miami to a government shelter. It was a 'secure' shelter. They said that meant close supervision and tougher rules. They warned us, 'Don't even think about trying to escape from here.'

I spent twenty-six days in that Miami shelter. We stayed in a huge tent. There were many bedrooms with super large bunk beds. All the kids were Latinos and minors. There were between fifty to sixty kids in that tent and half were boys and half were girls. There was a lady in charge and anytime we left the dorm rooms she had to escort us. When it was time for a meal half of the group would go to the cafeteria in another tent and the other half would stay with the group. We could get seconds and we ate five times a day, three meals and two snacks. They told us that we had to eat what was on our plate and that we needed to be full. We had to eat fast and finish in only thirty minutes. It was all American food and juice. We had a competition once to see who could drink the most juice boxes. I drank thirteen but one guy drank fourteen. He was everybody's favorite. He was really young and chubby and he was so funny.

They also gave us clothes at that place. If we tore the clothes, they told us to get a new one. I wore sandals for a week. My feet were so big that they needed to measure them to get me shoes. They gave me a medical and eye exam, wrote down my height and weight, and gave me vaccinations. Once a week I saw my caseworker but I would speak on the phone with a counselor. Other social workers explained about our rights, that we could talk to our mom. We had the right to have sufficient food and the right to complain if we were not happy. They talked about helping us get legal papers and said that they needed to gather information about my case. I told them about my past, why I came here, and I explained about my father and the threats I received. I got court dates and they explained that I had to attend those hearings and that my case was active. I go to each court appointment to get the judge to continue the case. I have still not seen an attorney."

Javier has been in the United States for two years. He is happy at home and at school. His friends are mostly Latinos because speaking English with his American friends takes him outside of his comfort zone. He admits to being shy and worrying about making a stupid mistake. He is in the ESOL track and claims to be doing well. In that class he stays away from the new kids who only speak Spanish because he knows how important it is to learn English. He likes his classes and says he is learning a lot. This is in part because of the close relationship he has developed with a teacher who also coaches him in soccer, "He is a gringo but he speaks Spanish and studied in Mexico. He is an excellent teacher. He helped me after I got injured on the field my first year and even took me to see a doctor." His teacher understood the challenges that he had adjusting to an American school and always got him back on track when he was down. He appreciates other teachers who are strict because, in Javier's words, "young boys get easily distracted and they need to get called out when they misbehave." His favorite classes are government and science.

Javier has big ambitions. He became interested in animal medicine by watching YouTube videos of veterinarians treating sick animals. Now he wants to go to vet school and learn how to treat large farm animals. He asks if I know what is involved. I do because my eldest daughter is a veterinarian. It requires eight years of higher education and excellent grades. I don't tell him that it is more difficult to be admitted to vet school than it is to enter medical school. I don't mention the expense or the impossibility of getting student loans without legal status. Despite his ambition, the odds of getting into a graduate professional school are against him. Javier does not fit the profile of famous Dreamers like José Antonio Vargas, the *Washington Post* journalist, or Karla Cornejo Villavicencio, who was the valedictorian of her class and wrote a best-selling book. They spent their early childhoods in the United States, mastered the language, and were high academic achievers with a bright future. It is unlikely that Javier will find a benefactor to provide high school tutors to help him enroll in college classes or to pay his tuition.

Javier lives in a mixed-status family headed only by his undocumented mother. Nohely explains that her husband was a very involved stepfather with Javier but is now stuck in Mexico working at odd jobs until he can get cross the border without getting caught. Increased interior enforcement by ICE in 2018 makes his safe travel across the country even more challenging. In contrast to his four sisters who were born in the United States and are citizens, Javier is undocumented and, as a result of his apprehension in Texas, is in removal proceedings in the

Arlington immigration court. The shelter staff explained that he might have an asylum case based on his father's murder by a drug cartel and his beating by a local gang. Yet, after eighteen months in the United States, Javier's mother has still not found a pro bono attorney to represent him in immigration court. Without his stepfather's wages, it is out of the question to hire a private attorney.

7

Elisa's Story

"In Our Family, We Have Lived Apart More Than We Have Lived Together"

We meet Elisa and her twelve-year-old son, Enrique, at a McDonald's restaurant near Herndon, Virginia. It is a short drive from where they live. We could not meet Elisa and Enrique at home because they rent a single room in a house and cannot have visitors. Elisa's brother drops them off and tells her to call him when our interview is finished.

2013

In our family, we have lived apart more than we have lived together. My husband came to the US to work in 2008 when our son Enrique was three years old. We were separated for more than four years before I came here in 2013 to join my husband. I left Enrique with my mother in El Salvador. That same year, in 2013, I got pregnant with our second child. My husband and I lived together for only one year but it was a happy one because we celebrated the birth of a baby girl. He got deported to El Salvador in 2014 when the baby was only two months old. My husband had not seen his son in five years. They spent six months together back home before we made arrangements for Enrique to come here. He came in 2015 but he only lived with his sister for five months before I had to send her back to El Salvador. Without a husband I couldn't care for her and work six days a week as a house cleaner. The daughter who was conceived and born here is now the one living with my mother back in El Salvador. Enrique and I are together in this country but he has no legal status. He is twelve years old and in middle school. We are once again a family divided between two countries.

In 2013, when I came here, my husband was working and I looked at a bulletin board with many different announcements about jobs. I didn't know English and had no papers so the only choices for me were to clean houses or take care of kids. The ads for cleaning houses required experience. When I called a cleaning company, I admitted that I did not have experience and they said that they would teach me. They took me on for three months. None of the other women had papers and thank God the boss didn't care. That first day on the job was really tough because I cleaned three entire houses. When I got home I had to lie down. My whole body ached and I felt feverish. When my husband came home, he saw me lying on the couch and said, "What's the matter? Why isn't dinner ready?" He wasn't happy about that but he took me out to dinner.

2015

My son was so happy to see his father when he was sent back to El Salvador. It was important for them to get to know one another again and for my husband, who was the only son in his family, to spend time with his mother. I was alone in the US with the baby and so our plan was for my husband to bring Enrique back with him in the spring of 2015. My husband and Enrique traveled together through Guatemala and Mexico but when they got to the border my husband arranged for Enrique to cross ahead with a guide. My husband didn't know it at the time, but they caught Enrique right away and sent him to a government shelter in Texas. My husband made it across but immigration caught him in Houston. They saw that he had no papers, had been charged with a felony in 2013, and was deported in 2014. Our plans collapsed when I got word that my husband was in jail and my son was also in custody. It was a terrible time for me because I was working two jobs, caring for my baby, trying to communicate with my husband, gathering information for his case, and filling out the paperwork required by the government before they would release my son to live with me. I was down to 105 pounds.

The problem my husband had with the law started when he was working to install carpets. His coworker was from Afghanistan and the boss had put my husband in charge. That man did not like taking orders from my husband. They got into a fight when my husband told him to empty the trash. He refused to do it and when my husband insisted he got angry and punched him. They both had sharp carpet cutters and when the Afghani pulled out his knife he cut himself. That stopped the fight but when the boss, who was also from Afghanistan, came to check on their work, the worker lied about my husband. He said that my husband had knifed him and showed him the wound. At that point the boss called the police and without much of an investigation, they charged my husband with assault. That was a huge problem because we needed to hire an attorney and we heard that a trial could cost between $10,000 and $12,000. We didn't have the money for that.

We turned for help to the pastors at our church in Annandale. One of the lady pastors called about fifty different attorneys until she found one who agreed to charge us $1,500 to represent my husband. The church donated half the fee and so we had representation. The lawyer advised us not to go to trial because if they found my husband guilty, he could receive a ten-to-fifteen-year prison sentence. So they had a hearing in court that lasted more than five hours. The boss gave testimony that favored the Afghan worker but there was no evidence to support his story. There were no fingerprints on my husband's knife or camera footage in the building. It was the Afghan's word against his. In the end the prosecutor agreed to remove the felony charges and to reduce his sentence to six months of jail time. He had already spent two months in pretrial detention while we were searching for an attorney. So he served four more months and in the end, they deported him.

After immigration caught Enrique at the border, he spent one night in a freezing cell at the Border Patrol station. The kids who came alone, like my son, were moved to cages the next day. Those cages were bigger but no warmer. He spent one night there before they transferred him to one of the government shelters. He had a social worker he could talk to but no lawyer. He had a photo of his sister that he kept with him but he didn't know if his father had made it across the border or where he was.

Enrique was allowed to call me once a week and I could text the social worker to ask her about him. She sent me papers to fill out so that he could be released. But in order to get him released I had to give the social worker a valid address. Because I was renting a room in a house, the landlord refused to let me use that address. I tried other people from my community but no one would let me put their address on the release papers. I didn't know what to do. I was desperate to get him out and have him come home with me. I was so worried because I really didn't know how he was being treated and why it was taking so long. So I went to the pastor of my church and explained the situation. He was renting a basement apartment to an elderly couple and he convinced them to let me use their address. By that time, Enrique had been in the shelter for a month.

So when they said yes, I filled out the papers. The government approved the release and then they told me that I would have to pay for his flight from Texas to Virginia. They only gave me one day to make the arrangements and to send the money. I had to borrow $1,000 for the trip because I had to pay for Enrique's ticket and for an escort since he was underage. I had no license and no car so I had to take a taxi with the papers to a business with a fax machine. I barely made it.

Although the process of releasing immigrant children from federal custody to a suitable sponsor has been framed in terms of the best interest of the child, the process served as a system of control closely tied to immigration enforcement and economic conditions. Immigrant parents and close family members were subjected to a humiliating process of scrutiny before they could be approved as sponsors for their own children. They were required to fill out complicated paperwork in order to verify the child's relationship with the family and to identify risk factors that might threaten a safe release. Decisions about release were determined as much by security considerations—legal status, criminal charges, or financial insolvency—as by emotional bonds and family connections. Federal staff frequently balked at releasing children to homes they deemed too small and overcrowded or to family who lived with unrelated adults in order to pool scarce resources. Why, families wondered, did the federal government insist that they pay expensive travel costs to be reunited with their children when it had detained them in the first place?[1]

So they released Enrique from that shelter and he started school in 2015. That November, when his baby sister was just one and one-half years old, I sent her back to El Salvador. I had no choice because I was working so much. Many families from back home are faced with the same situation. Small kids require so much attention and you don't get the same care from a babysitter. For them it is only a job for money. So my mother's sister got a travel visa to come to the US and she took my daughter back with her. The only good thing about that was that my husband was able to be with her to celebrate her second birthday. He had not seen her since she was two months old and he bought her a beautiful, white dress and toys. He was a good father to her and to my son. We have pictures of him holding her.

2017

In early 2017 my husband started having convulsions that were followed by a massive stoke. He could not move or speak. His sister took him to a public hospital where he developed a high fever and went into a coma. The fever stayed very high and his heart was barely beating. He died after three days. [sobbing] I couldn't go back to El Salvador to bury him because I have no status here and I couldn't leave Enrique. His father was the only son in that family. Now his mom will be alone with his nephew and his sister. I am alone as well.

The good part is that Enrique has adapted well to school and gets really good grades. This year he is in a regular science and history class, and has ESOL [English to Speakers of Other Languages] only for English. Science is his favorite now. Next year, in eighth grade, there will be no more ESOL. He wanted a computer but I couldn't buy it for him. So he saved all his gifts from my husband's cousins in Florida and Virginia and I added a little and we were able to get him one.

What will the future hold? My daughter is three and one-half years old now. I have applied for a place in Head Start for her with a social worker so I am ready to bring her back here. Because Enrique was apprehended and held in federal custody in Texas, that is where he first appeared in immigration court. His case was transferred to the immigration court in Arlington, Virginia, but when his court date came I didn't take him. I couldn't take him because I have no papers and no attorney. The judge gave him an in absentia deportation order. I don't have money and from what I have heard neither one of us can get legal status. So I figure that as long as he is not a problem in school, there will be no problem for him. He has a sister who is a US citizen so he will have to wait until his sister turns twenty-one and can petition for him to get legal status.

Elisa's understanding of immigration law is incomplete. Legal immigration to the United States occurs through a mixture of visa categories but there are only a small number of pathways to gaining legal status. Family relationships, ties to employers, and humanitarian protection are the major channels for immigrants seeking temporary or permanent US residency. Elisa refers to the family preference visas for relatives of US citizens. It is true that US citizens can sponsor adult children and siblings. However, immediate family members of US citizens have priority—spouses, unmarried children under twenty-one years of age, and parents. All other family relationships are subject to annual caps on the available visas. Sponsoring a sibling is a fourth preference category and is subject to additional limits on family visas depending on the country of origin. As of April 2019, the wait for US citizens to sponsor adult, unmarried children (in the first preference category) was more than seven years for most parts of the world and much longer for those from Mexico and Central America. There would be even longer waits for fourth preference categories such as siblings.[2]

At this point, I ask Enrique to tell us about his life in El Salvador and his trip to the United States. Enrique shared his story:

When I was in El Salvador, I lived with my mom's parents, her sister, and my little cousin. Then my dad and I left with a coyote to come here. They told me that the trip from El Salvador to the US border would take three weeks. I remember that the coyote was pretty good with us. He fed us and kept us away from the gangs and the migra. We mostly traveled at night and once we had to walk all night. I was so tired that my dad carried me on his shoulders. When we were close to the US we stayed in an abandoned house. The guide came to tell us kids that we would leave first and that it was time to go. I just wanted to leave and get it over with. So I jumped up and ran so fast, ahead of everyone. On the road I felt so bad because I realized that I had never said goodbye to my dad.

We got caught by the migra as soon as we crossed. They took us to a station near the border. It was not good because it was freezing and they only gave us an aluminum blanket for warmth. Then they transferred us to cages and we saw parents with small children there. I remember one lady with a small child who would not let go of her mom. I only stayed there one night and the next day the agent called my name and they took me to a shelter. I was worried about my dad and wondered if he made it across. I didn't find out 'til later that they deported him again. I spent a long time in that shelter. I made friends with four of the other kids.

I came here in May but I didn't start school until September. They put me in fifth grade and it was scary because I didn't know English and I didn't have any friends. Then they put me in a class with other kids who didn't speak English. I made friends with kids who understood some Spanish and they helped me. I really liked the English teacher because she taught me some vocabulary, and from the beginning, I liked math class.

Two years later things are so different. I can understand English and I feel good about school. I get really good grades—all A's and B's—more A's and B's than before. I am in the ESOL class for English but I take regular classes in science, history, and PE. Now my favorite class is science. Next year, when I am in eighth grade, I will be finished with ESOL classes. I wrote a story about my trip here from El Salvador. It was all in English. My teacher really liked it. I wrote it on my new computer. We started a gift fund last year and every time I got money from my cousins in Florida or from my uncle here in Virginia I saved it. My mom helped me and I was finally able to buy it.

Elisa and her husband's story is that of a couple deeply committed to one another and their children but forced to live apart. Unlike the other stories, there are no domestic violence incidents or threats from criminal gangs driving this Salvadoran family from home. Rather, both parents leave home to escape poverty and to seek better opportunities for work and education. A heavily militarized border, limited avenues for legal status, and an unforgiving labor market for the undocumented make it impossible for the family to live together on the same side of the border. When Elisa's husband fell ill and died, alone in a public hospital in El Salvador, she was unable to return to El Salvador and bury him. It is no small irony that the child without legal status is the one who will stay in the United States, while her child who is a US citizen was sent back to El Salvador to be raised by a grandmother. If Elisa is able to bring her daughter back to the United States, how will an undocumented single mother who rents a room and cleans homes for a living manage to support two children?

PART III

Living in the United States

8

The Parenting Classes

"Our Parents Don't Tell Us That They Love Us"

2017

Fairfax County, Virginia, is one of the nation's largest school districts, serving an ethnically and nationally diverse student population of 188,000 students in K–12 (kindergarten through twelfth grade) who speak over two hundred languages. Over a quarter of the students are economically disadvantaged[1] and learn English as a second language. The school district helps immigrant parents enroll their children in school and access social services. It also offers free family reunification and parenting classes for immigrant parents who have experienced long periods of separation from their children. The classes are the brainchild of Robin Hamby, an educator and family partnership specialist with the Fairfax County schools. Hamby designed a curriculum that addresses the special challenges of immigrant parents whose teenagers need support in adjusting to American life and schools. Immigrant instructors, who are bilingual and have raised their own children in the United States, lead the classes.[2]

Family Reunification Class

Eight parents attend the three-hour family reunification class on September 27, 2017. There are two instructors, both women, who take the participants through an exercise that requires making a sincere apology (*disculpa sincero*) to their kids. This activity draws explicitly on sociolinguist Deborah Tannen's work on effective apologies.[3] The exercise centers on admitting blame, realizing the harm caused, showing remorse, and promising never to repeat the action.[4] One of the instructors, Mary, assures the parents that, "There are no bad intentions but we as parents need to hear and recognize the hurt and sadness felt by our child when we left them behind. Saying that you sacrificed so much and work hard for them is not enough."[5] She divides the groups into pairs for a role-playing exercise. One plays the parent and the other the child and they use a prepared script. The parents read through it too quickly and the second instructor, Claudia, admonishes them gently, "The kids have to believe you. You have to tell them that you love them. You have to say it and repeat it." Her colleague, Mary, adds, "It is hard because for many years, you only talked on the phone with an app or on Skype. You and your children don't know one another and now you live together."

One mother waits until the other participants leave class before telling the instructors that she is unsure if she would be able to tell her children how she feels about them. When she was a child, her parents did not kiss or hug her and never once said that they loved her.

October 4

The third class is the best attended, with ten parents and their children. The school provides a free hot meal and the mood is upbeat. One of the night's exercises puts the young people in one room and their parents in another. Each group makes the outline of a person on brown paper and records their "deep feelings" close to the head, heart, and hands. Next to the heart, the mothers write, "Love of my child, Peace in the family, Family unity, and Faith in God." Next to the head, the parents record their dreams. They want to bring their other children to the United States. They want them to get good grades, take advantage of the opportunities in the United States, and maybe even become professionals. A longer list involves their fears. They worry that their children will not listen to them, will stop studying and drop out of school, or worse, will join gangs. They are afraid that they will lose a job and be unable to put food on the table or make the rent. They associate the hands with caring for their kids and helping them find work. One father writes, "I will be a good parent." A mother writes, "I hope that our kids will be able to do what we can't do." Under that sentence, another mother puts, "I don't want our kids to repeat the mistakes we made." When the teams come back together the parents read what they have written to their kids.

Then it is the kids' turn. Three of them speak up. Leisy and Melvin are seventeen and in the ninth grade and the third, Kevin, is fifteen and in the tenth grade. Leisy, separated from her mother for eleven years, makes a show of hugging her in front of the group. Everyone smiles but she and Melvin point out that the big problem is communication. They say that they don't talk much with their parents and when they try to share their problems, their parents don't listen. They want to live with their parents but don't feel loved. They worry about getting good grades. They think that studying is hard and finishing school will allow them to live better and to buy more things, like a TV.

Paulina Hidalgo, a senior director of the parenting program and a native Ecuadoran who came to the United States in 2001, comments on the family reunification class: "The kids cannot do well in school until their huge emotional burdens are addressed. They don't have a connection with their parents and when they have behavior problems in middle and high school, their parents don't know how to respond. The kids need to feel loved."[6] Her colleague, Mexican-born Susie Stratham, who has also been in the United States for twenty years, explains, "The parents initially refuse to take the blame. They insist that they did nothing wrong by leaving to come to the US. They say that they sacrificed so much for their kids and that they should be grateful. The kids say, 'You sent all that stuff but you were not there for me.' So, meeting them in the middle and creating a connection with a sincere apology is better than giving a long explanation with excuses."[7]

The Parent Project Class

The Parent Project class begins promptly at 6:00 p.m.[8] It meets weekly for ten sessions and is designed as a guide for the immigrant parents whose children attend the Fairfax County public schools. Because the parents and their children have been separated for long periods, the school anticipates conflicts in the home and significant problems adjusting to American life. Everything in the United States is different, from the language and the schools to the makeup of their families. The family may now include a new stepparent and younger half siblings who were born in the United States and have American citizenship. Working from a manual that focuses on "changing the harmful behaviors of teenagers," instructors use hypothetical scenarios, role-playing, and free discussion to help parents rebuild family relationships that are badly frayed. To entice the families to attend, the school district provides a free dinner and childcare for younger siblings.

October 25, 2017

The lesson on this evening focuses on the need to establish and enforce clear standards of discipline within the family. The mothers are reminded that active supervision is key so that their children know who is in control.

Mary says:
In our countries we have more family structure and supervision because we have our grandmothers and our neighbors to look out for our children. Here we feel like we lose control and our children are exposed to so many bad influences like drugs, sex, and violence online. The point is that you need to know where your children go when they leave the house and what they are doing. You need to find out who their friends are and where they live.

The workbook includes a cautionary tale about the need for vigilance. A father drives past the house where his teenage son is attending a party. To his horror, he sees teenagers passed out on the lawn, others obviously high, and police cars blocking the street. When his son gets home, he is drunk and is barely able to walk. His father delivers a lecture and grounds him. He wonders what would have happened if he and his wife had been asleep and not known about his misbehavior.

Amalia:
I always know where my son is because he calls me. In fact, this embarrasses him but he does it anyway.

Maria tells a story that makes all the mothers laugh:
My son wanted to go to the IHOP with his friends. I offered to drive him but he wanted to go in a taxi with his friends. So I followed them in my car to make sure that he actually went there. I was worried because he is a bit goofy and tends to fool around too much with his friends. I stayed in the car across from the restaurant the whole time until he called me to pick him up. He never knew I was there.

One mother says that her oldest son downloaded an app on her phone that allows her to track her other kids' whereabouts. Another mother mentions that her oldest son uses Snapchat to keep track of her other children. She explains:

That app allowed us to follow my younger son when he goes to a restaurant with his friends and when he leaves.

Mary jokes:
That woman has a private detective!

Mary repeats that parents should insist on meeting their children's new friends even if their kids don't like it. She says that trust is earned and it has nothing to do with supervision. She cautions the mothers that the largest consumers of internet porn are children between twelve and fourteen. "Kids use cell phones, not computers, to access the internet. Watch out if your child has a second cell phone. It could mean contact with a gang member or a human trafficker!"

One mother described confronting her teenage daughter over the sexual messages she found on the girl's cell phone:

When we were arguing my daughter pushed me so I slapped her. The next morning she left the house at 6:00 a.m. before anyone was up and didn't come back after school. I was too scared to call the police since I had hit her. So the whole family went to look for her and that night we found her at the mall.

Another mother volunteers that her children threaten to call the police if she hits them.

The second instructor, Claudia, explains that the police in Fairfax are there to help everyone—including immigrants. She adds:

The police will not arrest parents for hitting their children as long as there have been no past incidents involving the police or the parents do not cause injuries.

In the community, family dynamics and encounters with law enforcement can be much more complicated than this exchange suggests. A parent liaison staff member spoke about her work with immigrant families but insisted on not using her real name. She was born and raised in Brazil, is fluent in Portuguese and Spanish, and trained as a doctor before coming to the United States. She works in a Fairfax County high school where 56 percent of the twenty-two hundred students are Hispanic. She explained that while the Parent Project classes are helpful to many immigrant families, they are no panacea. The mothers are largely uneducated, have children in their teens, and become grandmothers in their thirties. Corporal punishment is something most of them experienced as children. Yet beating disrespectful sons and daughters while living in the United States can have unintended consequences. She described a case that she said that she would never forget:

A mother came to us because her daughter had a new boyfriend and she knew that it was a physical relationship. The mother suspected that her daughter was pregnant but really wanted her to stay in school. She came to me and asked how she should handle the situation. As a parent liaison, I am not supposed to make recommendations. She was a well-spoken woman who had a steady job in a cleaning business. So I sent her daughter to see a social worker and the next week the daughter had an abortion. At which point the mother beat the crap out of her. Then the girl's friend told the social worker about the beating and she had to report it to the police. When the police questioned the mother, her defense was, "Yes, I beat her because she was sassy and disrespectful." The cops arrested the mother and the girl's stepfather asked the social worker to remove the daughter from the home. She was only fifteen years old! I was with Child Protective Services when they took her and placed her with a wonderful foster family. She lived with them for two years and got back on track.

November 8, 2017

On this night in early November, the mothers are all Central Americans, except for one Peruvian woman. The topic is how to manage teenagers who act out. How do mothers control their kids given the cultural differences between home and the United States? What happens if their kids want to go out on a school night and don't do their homework? If they demand a cell phone or want flashy clothes? Or experiment with drugs? Or decide to have sex?

As the instructor begins class, Rosalía, an immigrant from an Indigenous Guatemalan community, takes her fussy eight-month-old granddaughter Jasmine, ties her in a wrap on her back, and rocks her to sleep. Rosalía, her daughter Ofelia, and baby Jasmine are class regulars. Although the class began in September, Rosalía speaks up for the first time. Her first language is Mam and her Spanish is not easy to follow but she speaks loudly and with authority.[9] She explains that she is the sole breadwinner for her Guatemalan and American families.

Rosalía:

I have a daughter in Guatemala who is fifteen. She lives with her grandfather and grandmother and my nephew and lately she is acting out. She refuses to get out of bed, she won't wash her clothes, and she does not want to attend school. I left my daughters with my mother and came to the US with my husband. Our son, Michael was born here in 2014. We worked hard and brought Ofelia here in 2016. My husband was a good father. He was strict and kept the children in line but he died this past June. Now I am a single mother. When I look back, I had no good examples to follow. My parents lived together but my father drank a lot and chased women. My mother never told me to take school seriously and to apply myself. That's why all I know how to do is clean. I tell my children all the time to study so they can have a better life than mine. I worry because my daughter in Guatemala only wants to spend time on her phone.

Mary:

Why does she even have a phone? She is too young. You need to set the rules and stop sending money if she acts out. She should not have access to the internet.

Another woman pipes up:

It is the same with my daughter who lives in El Salvador with my cousin. She wouldn't go to school so I threatened to stop sending money. I told her that if she stays home she will have to wake up early, wash dishes, do laundry for the neighbors, and cook for the whole family. That did it. After a week she went back to school and followed the rules.

Rosalía:

I told my daughter in Guatemala: "No more money for the internet. Try coming here and earning $100 if it is as easy as you think." That got her attention.

Another workbook scenario involves a mother who is shopping at the mall. She notices a group of girls who are wearing very revealing clothes. They wear see-through blouses and shorts that barely cover their bottoms and leave nothing to the imagination. The girls are no older than thirteen or fourteen, and the mother shakes her head in disbelief. She wonders how parents could allow them to dress in such a provocative manner. Suddenly, she notices that her daughter is a part of the group.[10]

One mother comments:
It is difficult because children have two faces. With us they have one face and with their friends they have another face.

Later this topic leads to a discussion of teenage love: *noviazgo entre adolescentes*. Mary warns the mothers about the risks of teenage relationships and lectures them on the need to monitor their behavior. She has one of the mothers read from the workbook: "One in five adolescent girls are victims of physical or emotional abuse at the hands of their boyfriends and less than 10 percent turn to parents for help. Given the heightened risk associated with early sexual activity, the increase in HIV and other sexually transmitted diseases, parents are right to establish stricter supervision and pay attention to the behavior of their teenage children and their relationships."[11]

How, she asks the class, should mothers manage teenage girls who want to go out with boys?

Maria:
I would show my daughter how to dress and to put on makeup. When these young girls put on glossy red lipstick to make their lips look bigger, it looks ridiculous.

The mothers talk over one another sharing stories about heavy makeup, low-cut tops, and skin-tight skirts. They agree that teenage girls want to act older than they are. One mother says that you have to keep an eye on them because you don't want any surprises. She means a teenage pregnancy. Another says that if her teenage daughter began having sex it would kill her husband and he would blame her for giving their daughter too much freedom. Another says that men are too uncomfortable to talk about sex with a daughter because they see them as little innocents.

The next day, my undergraduate research assistant, Eliana, sends me the picture of an iguana. Her Dominican mother, who is old-school, gave her the same lecture when she was in a New York high school. Her mother mockingly compared such girls to a lizard whose protruding red lips draw attention and send explicit messages.

December 5, 2017

After the dinner break, baby Jasmine fidgets and cries. Rosalía takes a spoonful of hot coffee, blows on it and gives it to the baby. From their looks and whispers it is obvious that the other mothers disapprove. Rosalía swaddles her tightly in a blanket and hands her to Ofelia.

The instructor begins the lesson by reminding the mothers that to rebuild a stable family structure they must have rules that are clear and reasonable. The children need to know who is in control. The workbook activity involves a teenage girl screaming at her father because he refuses to let her go out. Both instructors lead the class tonight—Mary and Claudia. Claudia often shares stories about raising four children in the United States, and she asks the mothers what they should do. Ofelia yells out, "I would tell her, 'You go for it, girl!'" The mothers laugh but Claudia's colleague, Mary, insists that such behavior is not acceptable.

Rosalía speaks up again, telling the class that Ofelia arrived pregnant in the United States and gave birth to Jasmine in March 2017, three months before her stepfather's death. She attends ninth grade in a local high school and is also causing problems. Instead of coming home after school she stays and hangs out with her friends. She forgets that she is a mother.

Rosalía:
I told her that she has to come straight home because I work and also take care of her baby. After that talk, she began to come straight home.

Suzie scolds Ofelia:
You cannot go out and be on the streets when you should be with your baby. It seems to me that you put yourself in this situation in the first place by going out and getting pregnant.

Mary ignores this comment but says:
It is your responsibility to take care of this baby, not your mother's.

Suzie whispers loudly to the women at her table:
If she takes care of that baby too often, you can bet that the daughter will bring another one home.

Mary introduces another hypothetical scenario involving a heated argument between a father and son. The teen is threatening to leave home because the rules are too strict. What should they do?

Ines:
To lower the temperature, I would tell my son: "This conversation will continue tomorrow."

Suzie:
If my son threatened to leave home, I would pack his bag and drive him to the bus station.

Rosalía:
At one point Ofelia threatened to leave home because I insisted that she help me and that she study harder. I told her that if she wanted to go she could but to leave her clothes behind since I bought them. I told her to behave because I pay the bills, I watch her baby, and I also support her sister,

my parents, and her uncle in Guatemala. She started to cry and said that she was sorry.

Ofelia is blushing and averting her gaze while Mary praises Rosalía: You may be very quiet, but you have learned a lot from this class.

Not all confrontations end with a teenager's apology or acceptance of adult authority. Another parent liaison staff member described a disturbing case involving a young man from Honduras who was apprehended after crossing the border. He was detained and then released from federal custody to his aunt's care because he had no other family in the United States.

> This woman attended the Parent Project class several years ago because her nephew had just arrived in the US. She had two children of her own who were born in this country. When her nephew started high school he was a problem from the beginning. He skipped school, got bad grades, became involved with a local gang, stole her rent money, and when she finally confronted him, he assaulted her. We knew that her nephew was a challenge but she never revealed these problems to us. What she should have done was to call the police and press charges. She never did that. Unfortunately, the lesson her nephew learned was that there are no consequences for his behavior.

An in-class activity follows. In this scenario, the father and child have a heated argument about teenage relationships. Both of them are getting angry. The mothers exchange knowing looks because this situation is all too common. The discussion groups are asked to make a list of bargaining tools to use with their children.

Ana:
I would tell my child which days that she could go out with her boyfriend. Then I would tell her that in return she has to help by doing chores.

Sandra remembered her grandmother saying that everyone who eats needs to work:

So I would tell my daughter that she must earn the right to spend time with her boyfriend.

Suzie:
Is it okay to tell my son that he is "the man of the house" so that he will accept more responsibility?

Several mothers weigh in:
"No, that is not a good idea."
"Absolutely not."
"That would cause problems!"

Mary explains:
You cannot do that because your son is only sixteen years old. He can't take on the kind of responsibility that would entitle him to be "man of the house." Instead, you could call him a man.

Rosalía:
Careful! If you call him the man of the house then he will tell you what to do (widespread laughter). My daughter in Guatemala told me that she was going to get a job so I would not tell her what to do. I told her, "Okay, fine you can be on your own." In three days, she was calling me and crying. I manage the household and take care of my son since my husband died. But if in the future he tries to tell me that what I have is his, I will tell him, "No. It is mine and you can leave if you want."

The mothers laugh.

As homework, the mothers are told to practice controlling their anger and to avoid yelling when disagreements arise.

Rosalía says to Suzie:
If you scream at them, they will not listen and it will just get worse. I used to yell at my daughter to do things and she would ignore me. But I changed my tone. Now she tells me, "Thanks mommy, you are right."

Suzie gets a laugh from the parents and instructors when she says:
Everyone, especially my ex-husband, tells me that every time I open my mouth I sound like I am yelling. But I didn't realize it until I recorded myself and then noticed that I really did sound like a nag.

A promotional video for the program features an immigrant couple, Miguel and Jessica, who credit the Parent Project class with helping them understand their children's feelings.[12] As a married couple who are well spoken in Spanish and English, Miguel and Jessica stand out among the regular class participants. Although school officials want both parents to participate, only mothers regularly attended the classes I observed in 2017–18. Fathers came sporadically, if at all. Although men are assumed to be the primary breadwinners and are always depicted as the heads of their families, the mothers also work long hours outside the home. They perform low wage labor and often hold down two jobs but are expected to manage the household and raise the children.

The mothers' attendance is sporadic and every week, there are late-comers to class because many rely on public buses for transportation. Most of the mothers are undocumented, speak no English, have little or no formal schooling, and struggle financially. They have smuggling debts to repay and, like Rosalía, support families in the home country. Because of the high rents in Fairfax County, they must share small apartments with extended family or friends where there is little privacy, no internet access, and no quiet place for their children to study.

Most of the mothers had been separated from their children for years before they were able to reunite. They are unprepared for the emotional roller coaster that begins when their children come back into their lives.

The children nurse deep anger and resentment for the years of separation. The mothers carry the scars of the abuse they suffered in the home country. Most had a baby as young teenagers, struggled with poverty, and were trapped in bad relationships that often lasted for years. They left home to escape the abuse but the cycle of unstable relationships, gender conflict, and economic insecurity continues in the United States. Although mothers may have increased autonomy in this country, they also experience continued male dominance. In the classes, they hear bewildering messages about how to raise and love their children. They are admonished to verbalize their feelings and to apologize for long family separations. Yet they wonder why their actions like working long hours for low wages don't speak louder than words. At the same time, instructors emphasize how important it is to establish their authority and to discipline wayward teenagers. Because of ramped up immigration enforcement in the county in 2017, they know that if they involve the police, they risk losing their children if they are apprehended by Immigration and Customs Enforcement (ICE) agents. Threatening to withhold monthly remittances to disobedient children in the home country could put an entire household at risk for food insecurity.

The mothers have all worked and paid taxes for years but most are not eligible for legal status. Not now, not ever. They live in the shadows and are trapped in a permanent limbo. The schools teach their children about the benefits of democracy and the rights of citizenship. These are rights they don't have but want for their children. Will their children be able to call this place home and have the normal life that their mothers sacrificed so much to give them?

9

Rosalía's Story

"They Don't Like [Indigenous] People Like Us"

We meet for the first time at Rosalía's Falls Church apartment on a bitterly cold afternoon in early January 2018. When we knock on the door, we hear Michael call for his mother and Ofelia opens the door. The boy is chasing a chicken—its wings are flapping, and, he warns in Spanish, it's "pooping like crazy." He says, "Too bad that you didn't come yesterday because we had two chickens. Then one flew out of an open window and we couldn't get him back." Michael scoops up the lone bird and shuts him in the bathroom while his half sister finds folding chairs for us to sit at the table. The small formica table is the only furniture in the living room except for a bare, single mattress pushed in a corner beneath a small wall-mounted TV tuned to a Spanish television channel. The wood floor is bare and worn. As we sit down opposite the small galley kitchen, a large cockroach scurries across the top of the table. Ligia motions for me to get my open purse off the floor. Michael is finishing a snack. He boasts that he is an uncle to Ofelia's baby and speaks three languages English, Mam, and Spanish. We say how impressed we are but Rosalía tells us that Spanish speakers on a public bus had recently mocked her for teaching her son a backward language like Mam: "They don't like [Indigenous] people like us. They think that we have no value."[1] As if to explain his father's absence, Michael suddenly announces, "My father died."

After Ofelia puts her baby down for a nap, she explains why she left Guatemala. Her mother came to the United States with her Guatemalan husband in 2009, leaving Ofelia and her sister with their grandparents in their Mam community in the Western Highlands of Quetzaltenango,

Guatemala. There were no plans to bring the girls to the United States because Rosalía's monthly wire transfers provided basic support for the extended family and paid the girls' private school tuition. Then, in 2015, she got a frantic call from seventeen-year-old Ofelia and immediately made arrangements to bring her to the United States. We learn that two successive generations of women were born of rape.

2015

In Guatemala, Ofelia always had issues with her grandmother. There was never enough food, never enough money, and constant reprimands for hanging out with her friends. Trouble started when she began to take a public bus to visit a school friend who lived in a nearby town. The bus driver was twenty-one and began to flirt with her, asking if she had a boyfriend. When she refused to talk to him, he wondered if she was stuck up. Did she think that he was ugly? When her friend gave the driver Ofelia's phone number he called, saying that he won her number in a lottery for pretty girls. The harmless flirtation stopped when he grew frustrated with her refusals.

Ofelia:

He said that he was sure I was a virgin and boasted about having had many virgins. I didn't even know what that word meant. He used dirty words for sex and I said that I didn't understand because I was just a girl. He said, "When I am your boyfriend, I will change that." Another time, I was on the bus alone after the other passengers got off. He stopped the bus, locked the doors and grabbed me, took my phone and said that he was taking me to a hotel. I said no and started to cry. He took me anyway and dragged me inside. The receptionist told him she would not take his money because I was resisting and crying. But in the end, she did. He kept saying, "Why don't you want me to be your boyfriend?" I said I needed to leave and go back to school. If I was late, the director would call my grandmother and I would get in trouble. But he forced himself on me and then he let me go.

I was so ashamed and I didn't want to return to school. He continued to call and taunt me saying he knew where I lived. He laughed about taking my virginity. Another time I took the bus and he was driving. He told me that we were going to spend a whole night together. I got so scared when he drove past several stops without letting any passengers on the bus. He only stopped when several men shouted to let them off. I jumped off with them and didn't stop running until I got to school. When my grandmother found out that I went to see the midwife at the local clinic, she figured out that I was pregnant. By that time everyone in town heard what had happened and there was gossip about me. My grandmother was furious and blamed me. She used bad words in our language and insisted that I abort the "evil spawn." When I told her that I wanted to keep the baby she took a stick and beat me so hard that I began to spot blood. I went to stay with my aunt who said that she really wanted to meet her new niece or nephew. Then my mother arranged for me to come here. The coyote was the brother of a member from our [Evangelical] church.

Mother and daughter grew up in San Juan Ostuncalco, a municipality located in the department of Quetzaltenango, where multiple forms of violence and inequality have a long history. During the thirty-six-year civil war in Guatemala, government forces used rape, torture, and murder as systematic tools of war against insurgent Mayan communities. Eighty-eight percent of those targeted for gender-based violence were Indigenous women and girls. Indigenous areas still have one of the highest rates of gender-based violence and killings in the country.[2]

In 2015, Ofelia was part of an epidemic of unintended pregnancies among young teenage girls in Indigenous areas in Guatemala.[3] To her grandparents, the pregnancy meant not only more hardship but also damage to the family reputation. In a tiny hamlet where gossip is a powerful weapon of social control, people said that Ofelia got what was coming to her. She was hanging out in the street, taking public buses without supervision, and flirting with strange men. Abortion is legal in Guatemala only to save a woman's life.[4] Despite the stiff restrictions on abortion and strong cultural opposition to it, ending a pregnancy is not uncommon in Indigenous areas. Researchers estimate that in these areas, there is one abortion for every five births.[5]

After a harrowing overland journey through Mexico and a hand-off to three different smugglers, Ofelia was apprehended on the Arizona side of the border. Rosalía was deeply shaken when a US Border Patrol agent called in the middle of the night to say that her daughter was in US immigration custody. The agent berated her: "Why did you send for her? It is wrong to bring kids across the border with a coyote. Don't you know that smugglers kidnap and rape young girls in Mexico? Who was the smuggler? Do you know that your daughter is pregnant? That she nearly lost the baby coming here?"[6]

Rosalía:
I said that I was sorry and that she came because my mother was abusing her . . . my own mom! I had trusted her to take good care of my daughter and she didn't. I told him that I was a good mother. I said that I could show him all the receipts of the wire transfers that I sent to Guatemala. I could prove that she was going to a private school and getting a good education. I was so afraid that they might not allow her to come to live with me. All I did was pray.

Ofelia spent forty-eight hours in a freezing cell in a Border Patrol station before she was transferred to a federal shelter for unaccompanied minors in Arizona. Rosalía immediately filled out the paperwork required for her daughter's release. Yet she faced another unnerving obstacle. After the required background check on all members of the household, federal authorities discovered that Rosalía's husband had an outstanding criminal charge in the United States. Rosalía knew but did not report that he had been jailed and deported in 2006 after his first wife had pressed charges for a domestic violence incident. Federal authorities rejected the family reunification request deeming the household unsafe for a pregnant minor. Rosalía resubmitted the paperwork, prompting further investigation of her fitness as a parent.

Rosalía:
The social worker was so angry that I lied at the beginning and I admitted that I was ashamed. I told her that I had never had any trouble with my husband and we had a young child at home. I said that I was afraid that we would get deported and that's why I didn't tell the truth. She promised to help but it was more than three months before the release was approved. The next social worker I worked with wanted all the paperwork on my son and then questioned whether I was able to care for my daughter and her new baby in my house. She read a list of baby items over the phone and asked if I had bought them. She assumed that I hadn't. I took a picture of the crib and sent it to her. I also had to prove that I could pay for the plane ticket to get her to Virginia from Arizona. It was so humiliating.

Ofelia spent three and a half months in detention before federal authorities finally approved her release. A departure date was set for New Year's Day. Yet, she was apprehensive because she and her mother had lived apart for seven years. Ofelia explained, "I took a plane to Virginia and I was really afraid. On the day I left I was so nervous that I couldn't eat. I didn't really have that much trust in my mom. I was ashamed because I was coming pregnant. When I was waiting for the plane, I even missed the shelter and the social workers."

2000
Rosalía grew up poor and worked as a young child. When her father drank, his kids hid from him. Both she and her sister left home at fourteen to live with their boyfriends. She got pregnant in 2000, the same year that she left home.

Rosalía:

When I was three months pregnant with Ofelia, my boyfriend left me to take up with another woman. He married her and they moved into a house in the same neighborhood. He never gave us anything—not money or food—but he did recognize the child as his. I was fifteen when she was born and had to leave school to work. The only work I could get was grinding corn and doing laundry. After I weaned her I had a chance to work at a busy market stall selling fruit in a town on the coast. It paid more but it was in a dangerous area with gangs and crime. I went despite the danger because I wanted to earn more. One day four men came to the stall and tried to take advantage of me. I screamed and they ran off but later they came back and dragged me behind the tables and abused me. I became pregnant with my second daughter and returned to my parents' home. Several years later I met my husband. He lived in the same area and saw me with my young daughters. He liked that I worked hard and took care of my family. I liked that he made a decent living and had built his own house.

Visible and invisible forms of violence still disproportionately affect Guatemalan women who are poor and Indigenous. They experience discrimination and persistent inequality in obtaining access to health care, reproductive services, education and employment. In the Western Highlands, most Indigenous families engage in some form of subsistence agriculture but men inherit and control ownership of land and other resources. Indigenous women constitute nearly 90 percent of the informal economy and on average have only four years of formal schooling. There are high fertility rates, high rates of infant mortality, and low life expectancy.[7] As a result of poor access to pre- and postnatal care, the rate of 110–290 maternal deaths per 100,000 live births in the Indigenous population is nearly three times higher than in the non-Indigenous population.[8]

Patriarchy was a fact of life in Rosalía's rural hamlet. In these communities, abusive men enjoy widespread impunity thanks to a sexual double standard reinforced by the media, law enforcement, and the justice system. There is widespread tolerance for alcoholism, infidelity, and domestic violence because they are viewed as normal behaviors for men.[9] There is a consensus about a man's right to abandon or abuse a "bad" wife or girlfriend but that a woman's role is to put up with maltreatment. The vast majority of gender-based crimes are underreported and go unpunished.[10] In a barrio where male misbehavior was often the norm, Rosalía's boyfriend paid no social price for abandoning her when she became pregnant at fourteen or for failing to support their daughter. In contrast, Rosalía had to quit school, return home, and scratch out a living selling food. Her brief quest for independence in another town ended with her rape, a second pregnancy, and a damaged reputation. In a town where female respectability confers important social capital, the perception of loose morals has serious consequences for finding and keeping a partner. As the single mother of daughters by two absent fathers, Rosalía sought to cultivate a positive image by avoiding men, working hard, and devoting herself to her children. She began a second relationship with a local man only after he determined that she was a respectable person and a good mother. Rosalía described her rape in a matter-of-fact tone but her voice trembled when she described how a US Border Patrol agent implied that she was a bad mother for smuggling her pregnant daughter to the United States.

After Rosalía and her partner arrived in Virginia, she had a series of precarious, low-paid jobs. First, she cleaned houses for a Salvadoran man who insisted she work without pay until she learned the job, and then paid her forty dollars a day to clean four houses. Another employer doubled her salary but was verbally abusive. She lasted one week and then found better-paid work washing dishes in a restaurant. After some months, she landed a job she loved caring for the baby of an American family. But when she got pregnant with her son, her husband refused to allow her to work outside the home. She quit that job but began to sell the lunches she made in her own kitchen, earning almost fifty dollars a day. Now that she has to care for two young children, her son and granddaughter, she still works from her home.

Rosalía never learned to read and insisted that Ofelia enroll in ESOL (English to Speakers of Other Languages) classes and continue her education as soon as she arrived in the United States. By that time, Ofelia was almost eight months pregnant. Her fellow students were curious about the pregnancy, and helped her locate classrooms, understand the grading system, and identify the strange cafeteria foods. But being in school with "a big stomach" made her self-conscious. She was completely lost in ninth grade English and Math but was afraid to ask questions. Worse still, she couldn't understand the Spanish spoken by her ESOL teacher. None of the sixteen students were Indigenous or from Guatemala. When her daughter was born in early March she decided not to return to school until the next fall.

Ofelia:
I had to repeat ninth grade English. In the fall, when I returned to class, I finally began to understand the language. I have a really good English teacher now and I got an A. We are learning the parts of speech. We choose books to read and then talk about them. We also learn civics and how the government works. We learn who the presidents were in the past. That is helpful but I want to talk more about the present and about Trump. He hates immigrants and wants to throw us all out."

Rosalía boasts about Ofelia's school performance and has her show off her English by reciting the three branches of American government and telling us the grades she earned. Ligia advises her to keep working hard because without a high school diploma, she would find only poorly paid jobs. Knowing how stretched the family budget was, Ligia suggests that Ofelia get a part-time job on Saturdays at the local 7/11. Rosalía firmly dismisses this idea, "She does not have a work permit. Besides, I did not bring her here to work. She will finish high school and get a good job."

Ofelia chose to keep her baby despite the violence of the conception. During another visit she reflects on her new life and the choices she made.

It is so different here than at home. Back there we were always out with people we knew. Here everyone stays inside and activities are planned. In Guatemala I went to school, came home, did my homework, and then went out on my own. Here we can't do a lot of things. Friends organize outings outside and I can't go. They have parties and I can't go. My friends say that it is so cute to be a mother but I am too young. I should be able to enjoy my youth and not have to worry about a kid until I am older.

During another visit some weeks later, Rosalía reveals that the man who raped Ofelia is now living in Atlanta. He found Ofelia on Facebook and has her cell number. He is threatening to report her to ICE and to take the baby away unless she allows him to see his child. Rosalía blocked his calls but thanks to Facebook he knows that they live in Northern Virginia and has a photo of Ofelia and the baby. What can they do? Get a restraining order? We hesitate to advise her given the risks of involving law enforcement now.

Just a few days after that visit, Rosalía calls Ligia late in the evening. One of her cousins, also without papers, was arrested in Richmond, Virginia, after a loud altercation with his Guatemalan housemate. He has spent two weeks in jail and needs money for bail. The court hearing is the next day and they need a ride to Richmond. Rosalía plans to go and to take both kids with her. It is out of the question to leave her cousin to face a US judge on his own. Family members in Guatemala and the US have pooled resources to pay the bail. They fear that her cousin could be transferred to ICE custody and then deported. Neither Ligia nor I are available to drive them to court. We never hear the outcome of the case.

Ofelia turned eighteen in 2018. It was a bad year for the undocumented. Fairfax County officials had largely resisted the harsh crackdowns on illegal immigration by the Trump administration that began in 2017. Initially, county officials maintained a progressive approach to this population, foregoing enforcement partnerships with federal authorities, working with local law enforcement to assist undocumented families in crisis, and supporting expanded support services. In Parent

Project classes, instructors repeatedly told the mothers that they had nothing to fear from local law enforcement. Yet over the 2017–18 school year, there were reports of immigration sweeps near schools, community centers, and churches, high-profile raids at workplaces, and mounting apprehensions during required check-ins at federal buildings. The heightened enforcement measures by the Trump administration created a climate of intensified fear in the county. Many mothers were simply too afraid to speak to us and kept their children indoors after they returned home from school. In fact, one evening, the Parent Project class at one Fairfax high school was canceled when school authorities saw ICE officers in vans just outside school grounds waiting to apprehend the undocumented families who came to pick up their children.

Those who were arrested at check-ins faced swift detention and deportation. Many of those families were mixed status, where one or more members had legal papers. After the arrest and detention of undocumented parents, their children—whether US citizen or undocumented—faced the choice of following deported family members to countries they left as children, remaining in the United States with extended family or friends, or entering foster care after deported parents lose their parental rights.[11]

A Fairfax County parent liaison staff member who preferred to remain anonymous described a vicious cycle that was not addressed in the Parent Project class but surfaced regularly in the school and in the community. Women were abused in their home country by family, neighbors, or gangs, had a baby in their teens, and had a bad relationship with their partner. They left home to escape the abuse, but the cycle continued in the US with them and their daughters.[12] The parent liaison explained: "I had the case of a fifteen-year-old who has a two-year-old and is pregnant again. I found her sobbing in the girl's bathroom soon after she came here. She and the baby's father had crossed together and were separated by immigration. He went to LA and she came to be with family in Virginia. A few months later, she began living with another boy and got pregnant a second time. We got a social worker involved because she has two kids and has to make something of her life. She was failing in school."

Despite Rosalía's ambitious plans for Ofelia, the odds of success are against her. Both Rosalía and Ofelia have been deeply marked by domestic and sexual violence. They are like many Central American women who are caught in a vicious cycle of intergenerational abuse—sexual assault or domestic violence in the home country. They leave their home country to escape the abuse and begin a new life but the cycle continues in the United States when their daughters get pregnant at a very early age.

It is unlikely that Ofelia will find a benefactor to provide high school tutors, to help her enroll in college classes, or to pay her tuition. In 2018, she was an eighteen-year-old ninth grader with a baby who had no support from a father or a partner. The man who raped her and fathered her child began to stalk her online from inside the United States. She lives with an undocumented single mother who cobbles together an income from work paid in cash, Medicaid benefits for her US-citizen son and granddaughter, and $500 a month from a cousin who pays to sleep on a single mattress in the living room. That money helps Rosalía cover the $1,200 rent for their run-down two-bedroom walk-up, but she must still pay utilities and cell phone fees. Since her husband's death she worries constantly about having enough money to support her families in the United States and Guatemala. She does not qualify for legal relief but is determined to scrape together $5,000 in attorney fees so that Ofelia can petition for a SIJS visa that would put her on a path to citizenship and a better life in the United States. Yet even in the United States, Rosalía and her children could not escape the stigma of their Indigenous status when they interacted locally with other Central Americans.

10

Vania's Story

"Who Is This Woman?"

The atmosphere is tense when Ligia and I arrive to meet with Vania and her youngest daughter in 2018. Eleven-year-old Gisell has recently arrived from El Salvador and has been enrolled in the fifth grade. Vania lives in a small two-bedroom walk-up with Gisell and four other family members. Vania and her two daughters, Gisell and Michele, all sleep in the largest bedroom, a niece and her husband share the second, and their young cousin, newly arrived, sleeps on the one of the two couches in the living room. There is no other furniture. The reunion with Gisell was not going well because it had been nine years since she lived with her mother. Although it is 3:45 in the afternoon, Gisell is still not dressed and refuses to come out of the bedroom. We wonder if she is sick. Vania shakes her head in exasperation and explains that Gisell has shut down emotionally.

Vania explains, "She refuses to speak to me. She has no interest in anything. She never brings home schoolwork. When she gets home she locks herself in the bedroom and watches TV soap operas for hours or she and her sister play loud music." Vania asks Ligia, "Why don't you go and see if you can get her out of bed? I tried already."

Ligia coaxes Gisell to come out. Sparrow thin, she wears pajama bottoms, a sweater turned inside out and her dark hair is a tangle of knots. She perches on the far side of the opposite couch and stares at the floor. We explain why we came and, as with all the families, we offer her a gift card. What she would like to buy? What would make her happy? Gisell begins to cry and answers in a whisper:

Nothing in this country makes me happy. I miss my grandmother so much. She was the one who raised me and showed me love. I want to be with her and my [three] sisters back home. I miss my friends and my cousins. We walked to school together every day. We would sing and laugh all along the way. The kids at school here don't talk to me. Even the ones who speak Spanish ignore me. I have no friends. I just want to go back home.

Vania interjects:

School back there [in El Salvador] is part of the problem. She had to walk twenty minutes to her school. They passed through neighborhoods that are controlled by gangs. What would she do when she finishes elementary school? There are no secondary schools in our town.[1] She wouldn't be able to go to another town by herself. It would be much too dangerous.

Vania began to make migration plans for her daughters in 2015, the year that El Salvador had the highest homicide rate in the world at 104 homicides per 100,000 people,[2] the highest concentration of gang members per capita in Central America,[3] and the highest rate of femicides.[4] Gangs are suspected of carrying out most of the 3,662 registered disappearances and abductions, a third of which affect women and children.[5] Gang-related violence and intimidation drive internal displacement in the country and contribute to poor school attendance. Twenty-eight percent of Salvadoran youth, those aged fifteen to twenty-four, do not attend school, work, or receive vocational training.[6]

Gisell is hunched over and sobbing softly. Ligia slips her arm around her and explains why she is in Virginia: "Your mother wants to protect you from the violence back home. Gangs and cartels make life so insecure. Here the schools are safe and the teachers care about their students. If you and your sister graduate from an American high school you will have a better future. There are few good jobs and so much poverty back home. A Spanish-speaking counselor can help you to enroll in after-school programs."

Vania says, "We know about the after-school programs but when they wanted to sign her up, I had to say that there is no point since she won't participate. I try to make plans with her when I am not working but she never wants to do anything with me."

Gisell's head snaps up and she glares at her mother, saying, "You are never here. The only things my sister and I do is clean this apartment."

We ask if they would consider attending the family reunification class offered by the school district? It was created for families like theirs who live together after years of separation. Vania likes the idea of the class, but it conflicts with her night job. Gisell rejects it out of hand, "I don't want to go to a class like that." Gesturing to her mother, she says, "I don't know who this woman is. She sent me back when I was so little that I hardly remember anything about this country. I don't have a father. I have no family here. My family is in El Salvador."

No one speaks for several minutes.

Vania begins her story:
I have five daughters. I was still a young woman when I was left a widow by one man and then abandoned by another. The father of the two oldest died when they were little and the father of the next two went to work in Colorado. After a year, he stopped sending money or calling us. We haven't heard from him since. Out of the blue one day in 2004 my grandmother contacted me to say that my father wanted to talk to me. It was a total surprise because he had never been a part of my life. He had left the country years ago and I heard that he married a US citizen and was living in California. At the time, I was working as a domestic in El Salvador. I was the maid, doing everything for the family, cleaning, cooking, and taking care of their baby. They paid so little but I needed the work. I had no husband and four children—three under eight—to support. So my father called back and said that he wanted me to come to the US. He had just sold a house and would lend me the money for the journey. I suppose that he wanted to make up for not having supported me as a child. At first I said, "No." I was so scared because of the stories

that I heard about women who get kidnapped, raped, and killed. I knew about the danger.

So later the same afternoon, my father called me at the boss's house and said, "You are coming here." I said, "Wait, I don't know. What about my daughters?" He said, "No. You are leaving tonight. I talked to your mother and she will take care of your kids." The boss was not at home but her sister was there. She overheard me and said, "Go ahead. Take your chances. With the pittance you make here, you will never be able to provide for your children." I was conflicted and my heart was troubled. My mom said she would keep my kids and not to worry. Then the night came. We agreed that we would not tell anyone in case I got caught and sent back. That meant I could not say goodbye to my oldest child who was at my aunt's house. She was eight years old and her sisters were five, three, and just six months old.

Mothers like Vania, who work as domestics and have little or no financial help from the fathers of their children, migrate to provide the necessities families lack: ample food, decent clothes, and school tuition. They turn to their mothers to assume the responsibility for the care of their grandchildren despite the hardships it imposes on them. When they migrate, mothers cannot raise their young children even as they provide material benefits children would not have if they stayed home. Regular remittances mean survival for the family in the home country. Yet without legal status or job skills mothers struggle to stay afloat. Vania lives in expensive Fairfax County in Northern Virginia and has to pool resources with three family members in order to make ends meet. Fourteen years after coming to the United States, she is doing the same unskilled work for low wages that she did in El Salvador. She pays taxes but has no benefits. She is illiterate in Spanish, speaks no English, and is ineligible for legal relief. Despite working two jobs, cleaning a gym five afternoons a week and an office two nights a week, she can barely support her family members in the United States and in El Salvador.

Gisell abruptly jumps up and hands back the gift card with an emphatic, "No thanks." Without looking back, she shuts herself in the bedroom. Her mother starts to cry. Vania says:

It is so difficult right now. She is acting out. She gets home and goes straight into the bedroom. She only eats junk food and drinks soda, throws wrappers on the floor, piles dirty plates in the sink, and plays music so loud that the neighbors complain. When I go into the bedroom she piles things all around her bed so I can't see her. The only time she smiles is when I leave for work. When they were in El Salvador, I was the one who always sent the money for food, clothes, and school fees. Now I get it from both sides. They complain about not having clothes or phones here. Then I have my mother constantly asking for more money because she says that there is not enough food to give my girls back home.

When their daughters migrate, grandmothers both gain and lose. They gain the love of grandchildren as they take on the mother role in families with absent parents. Gisell claimed to have only one mother—her grandmother. Yet her grandmother also gained a financial lifeline from the money that Vania sent every month. Although those funds were often stretched thin among members of a multigenerational household, the money pulled the family out of extreme poverty. At the same time, a grandmother's economic vulnerability and dependence on her daughters is linked to the persistent failure of fathers to support their partners and children. Mothers and grandmothers, as usual, carry the long-term burden.[7]

2004

In 2004, I came to this country to work and support the four daughters I left in El Salvador. In August of that year I started a journey that nearly killed me. During the twenty-eight days it took to get to the border, Mexican immigration caught me three times. They jailed me twice and then, unexpectedly, released me with no explanation. At one point I joined a group at the guest-house used by the smuggler in a desert town right on the Arizona border.[8] I don't know what town it was but they said many migrants pass through there. Our group set out to cross the border at night, but we met armed men who lie in wait for migrants. Those men assaulted me and took the little money we had as well as our watches and shoes. We knew that this was to confuse us and to make our trip through the desert longer and harder. What do I remember? Feet shredded by sharp stones, wild animals passing nearby, the numbing cold at night, and blindly following the smuggler. I heard that smugglers never tell migrants where they are or how far they have to walk. It is easier to keep them in line that way. Well, the same night that smuggler slipped away without a word. People panicked when they found out and the group broke up. Only two of the original thirty—me and a Honduran man—crossed into Arizona together. We escaped detection from la migra and followed along a dirt track on the US side. We were exhausted and famished, when we stumbled upon a run-down church. The Pentecostals who ran it gave us food, shelter, and helped us contact our relatives.

2006

You see, I met Gisell's father in 2006. We were both working at a Chinese restaurant in San Diego. He was from my part of the world—Guatemala—and I was lonely. We started to live together and soon I got pregnant. Gisell was born that year and I had three months to be a full-time mom. I had never been able to stop work to care for my other children. I loved that time—bathing her, holding her, feeding her. But I had to go back to work full-time because her father was drinking all his wages. I got a night job cleaning offices and needed his help. He refused to watch her because, he said, giving her a bottle and changing diapers was women's work. So I had to pay a babysitter. When he drank he would insult and beat me. The screaming made the baby cry. Finally, when she was twenty months old I couldn't take it and I sent her back to my mother. I separated from the father then and we have not heard from him since. My father and step-mother live in San Diego and I stayed with them for a few months after I crossed. Then I came to Virginia to be near my brothers and three of my nephews. All of them are relatives on my mother's side. Although he helped me I am not close to my father's family.

A year after I sent Gisell back to El Salvador I wanted her to return here before her US passport expired. My mother just flatly refused. She said that when she is in the US she stays indoors all the time, she has babysitters who are not good, she would suffer there. I waited and wanted to bring my older daughters here in 2016 because I was more settled but that has not worked out. Only the second oldest agreed to come here. Then I arranged for Gisell to come. I found out through my sister that my mom would not call me because she was angry that I did not ask her if Gisell could leave El Salvador. Maybe I do understand her feelings because she raised the girls. I guess that is why my girls act the way they do.

Grandmothers lose when their daughters leave and they become mothers for a second generation. They become caretakers for young children who often live with them in impoverished neighborhoods that have no electricity, sewers or running water. Their roles are temporary and insecure since most mothers migrate with the goal of bringing their children to the United States. Although grandmothers are expected to accept that their grandchildren will join their mothers, the decision can cause resistance and conflict. As their sole caregiver for twelve years, Vania's mother was fiercely devoted to her five granddaughters. She headed a large household with no financial help from the children's fathers. With the income she received from Vania she managed well. She zealously guarded this prerogative.

There is another awkward silence. We hear loud music from the bedroom and Ligia suggests a meeting with a school counselor. Vania insists that she has tried this, and Gisell brushes it off saying, "Why talk to people from that school? It doesn't matter."

Vania continues:
I want my girls to do well in school but I don't ever see them studying. When it was time for the book fair I didn't have any money. So I saved quar-

ters to buy them winter coats instead. Weeks later, I checked and the quarters were gone. I found out that Gisell had taken the money and bought books at the fair but never told me. That hurt me so much. What will I do about Gisell? I want she and her sister to get an American education. I don't want them to have to work two jobs as a cleaner like me. Gisell was born here. She is a US citizen. Why should I send her back now? I had no choice before. She is not doing well but if I send her back now she would win. I can't do that and I won't.

It is late afternoon and we prepare to leave as the other family members begin to return home. Gisell is still locked in her room. We ask if Vania has found legal representation for her older daughter Michele. She came to the United States in 2016 and turned twenty that year. Although she could petition for a special juvenile visa claiming abandonment by her father, Michele is ineligible for this form of legal status in a Virginia family court because she is over eighteen. An immigration attorney informed Vania that she could move the case to Maryland where eligibility for the SIJS was extended to twenty-one years of age.

Faced with ongoing economic insecurity and the changes in her daughters' lives, Vania's dream of reuniting with all her daughters collapsed in 2016. In the intervening years, the eldest left school, began living with her partner, and became pregnant. Her third daughter, then sixteen, has a learning disability and, after repeating several grades, was placed in the same high school class as her thirteen-year-old sister. In contrast, her second daughter, Michele, eagerly agreed to come to the United States. When Michele left home with a smuggler known to the family, her grandmother was bereft. She well remembered what had happened to Vania in Mexico. Her fears seemed justified when Michele was apprehended after crossing the border, detained in a federal shelter in Texas, and placed in removal proceedings in an immigration court. Vania was terrified that her mother would compromise Michele's release from federal custody. When a social worker from the shelter contacted Vania's mother, she was argumentative and insisted that her granddaughter should never have left El Salvador. Michele landed in federal detention for unaccompanied minors just ten days before her eighteenth birthday. If her release had been delayed, Michele would have been transferred to an adult immigration prison immediately after turning eighteen and subjected to harsh detention conditions.

When Gisell's turn came to leave El Salvador, her experience was very different. She could travel freely with her US passport. Unlike her older sister, Michele, she flew to the United States and was spared the dangerous land journey through Mexico as well as apprehension by Border Patrol and federal custody. Nonetheless, her grandmother vehemently opposed Gisell's departure and railed incessantly about the pitfalls of life up north. In the end, her grandmother did not stand in the way but she was a major factor in Gisell's refusal to accept her new life.

Like her youngest daughter, Vania has her own history of loss and trauma. She was abandoned twice by the fathers of her children and left without their support. When her own father belatedly reentered her life, his help was gratefully accepted but totally unexpected. He dictated the terms and conditioned her departure on her mother's willingness to care for her daughters. It came with no promise of monetary support for his granddaughters. Her journey across Mexico was marked by a series of violent arrests, detention in squalid Mexican jails, abandonment in the Sonoma desert and, most probably, sexual assault by border bandits. Although she lived for a number of months with her father and stepmother, conflicts arose. The emotional bonds with her father were frayed and she ultimately left California to live near her mother's relatives in Virginia. Having five daughters from three fathers provided no economic security, nor did it ensure a durable relationship. In all these relationships, she suffered domestic abuse and repeated abandonment. Her commitment to her children meant that she had to love them from a distance and then suffer their anger and rejection when they finally reunited.

Gisell suffered from her own sense of abandonment and displacement. She did not speak the language or feel that she belonged in a country where she holds full citizenship. Given the powerful ideologies surrounding motherhood throughout Central America, the care of relatives, even grandmothers, is no substitute for a parent. When asked about his parents, a young Salvadoran said to the interviewer: "I don't know who these people are! I am sorry if you feel I'm an ingrate . . . and you're going to tell me about their sacrifice and blah blah blah. I know the story. And I'm sure you'd side with my mother because she's such a hard worker [*rolling his eyes*] and loves me and all that. But I am not and will not be grateful to them for having sent me back."[9]

In this story, there are no celebratory images of family cohesion or the possibility of sanitizing the suffering and pain of the grandmother, mother, and her daughters. They are, and will remain, a transnational family connected primarily though cell phones and social media. In spite of the conflicts and challenges, distance has not shattered their ties to family. Remaining committed and connected to families across borders is less a matter of culture than a survival mechanism in places where, as Karla Villaviciencio says, "the ground has never quite seemed solid beneath our feet."[10]

11

Teresa's Story

"How Could This Happen Again?"

We meet Teresa and Sonia at the Bucknell Elementary School in Fairfax County Virginia on a late afternoon in February 2018. In addition to Ligia, Sonia's mentor, Marcia, joins us. Teresa begins her story.

2013

I had no papers in the beginning and I worked two jobs to save the money to bring my daughter Sonia from El Salvador to the US in 2013. The trip to Virginia took seventeen days and cost $13,400. That was much more than I expected so I had to borrow over $9,000. But I kept my promise that we would only be separated for a year. I used an American smuggler who ran a big operation using fake IDs, local guides, and safe houses along the route. She also paid certain US immigration officials at the border to turn a blind eye when her clients wanted to enter the US with false papers. Things went well until my daughter got to a safe house on the Mexican side of the border. Sonia was supposed to cross on a day when one of the agents on her payroll was on duty. But he didn't show up for three days straight. Meanwhile, the Mexican woman who was watching Sonia demanded more money and threatened to leave. She began to be abusive, screaming at her and refusing to prepare meals. So the plan changed. Sonia would have to cross the Rio Grande late at night with a group of other migrants. I was so afraid because I remembered how dangerous my own crossing had been.

2011

I had ridden the cargo trains through Mexico and nearly died when I was swept off the top, slammed into a tree and then fell ten feet. I was covered in bruises, shattered the bones in my foot, and even lost my memory for a time. Someone helped me to get to a migrant shelter close to the border that was run by a priest. Even though migrants can only stay for a few days, I was in such bad shape that he said that I could stay for a month. He had so little food that we ate pinto beans every day. I can't even look at beans now.

Migrant shelters close to the border are very dangerous spaces. People who are on the payroll of cartels, gangs, or human smugglers work in the shelters to gather information and troll for new recruits.[1]

The priest also arranged for me to cross on foot with a group of men and women from Mexico and Guatemala. After seven hours walking through rough terrain I couldn't keep up and the smuggler abandoned me. He left me with a little water and said to walk toward the light. If I sensed that an animal was close, I was supposed to lie down and not move. I knew that there were snakes, scorpions, and even mountain lions. Soon it was pitch black and I was out of water. I was walking blind and lost my footing on loose rocks. I grabbed a branch to break my fall and a long thorn pierced the palm of my hand. I had no idea how much time went by. Suddenly there was a helicopter overhead and lots of lights. It landed and people in uniform who spoke Spanish told me not to move. That was August 4, 2011.

They took me to a hospital where an immigration officer handcuffed me to a bed and stood guard. I didn't mind being in a clean bed with nurses to care for me and orderlies to bring me food. Two days later another officer came to interview me. Then I was shackled and taken to a prison. I asked him why I needed to be in chains since I was already restrained. He said that it was the rule in federal custody. When I got to the prison they gave me a prison uniform to wear and took away my pain medication. There were many rules in that prison. The day after I arrived they sent me to solitary confinement in a freezing cell for a whole day. My offense was breaking the rule against physical contact with another inmate. I didn't know that there was such a rule so when I recognized a friend from home I ran to hug her.

Even before the rapid expansion of the for-profit immigration prison system in 2014 during the Obama administration, immigration detention centers were the subject of repeated complaints of due process violations, unsafe conditions, and the rampant mistreatment of people detained there. Although it is technically a civil detention system, the conditions in immigration prisons are worse than in many state and federal prisons. There is little oversight, no meaningful grievance procedures, no limitations on the length of detention, and serious human rights abuses. The rules are arbitrary and the punishments are harsh. Basic medical care is woefully inadequate, the water is barely potable, and the food is so bad that to stave off hunger immigrants must buy their own at inflated commissary prices. A majority of immigrants in detention must appear in removal proceedings without attorneys because there is no right to funded legal representation.[2]

The memory of my crossing terrified me but I had to go along with the coyota's plan. I explained on the phone to Sonia that she should go with these people and that we would be together soon. I did not tell her how dangerous it was. In the end the smuggler paid a young man to carry my daughter on his shoulders across the river. He handed her off to a driver who took her to the smuggler's home outside Houston. It was a huge house and Sonia thought that all Americans lived like that. Then I faced another demand. I had to pick her up in Houston or pay extra to get her to Virginia. I couldn't leave work so the coyota hired two young men to drive thirty-six hours straight from Houston to the parking lot of Fairfax Hospital. That is where I met them and exchanged nine one-hundred-dollar bills for my daughter.

2013

I ask Sonia what she remembers about the journey from El Salvador to the United States.

Sonia:

My mom planned to bring me here a year after she arrived. I was really young—six years old—and I only remember bits and pieces about leaving El Salvador. She arranged for a Mexican couple to meet me and act like my parents to get me through Mexico. I remember crying and being afraid when I saw them. The man smiled at me and said, "Say hi to your mom." He was with a woman who seemed really nice. She knelt down and kissed me. It was so strange because they seemed to know me already. They knew what I liked to eat, what made me laugh, when I went to bed. The first thing they did was to give me a video game. That was amazing and I spent hours playing with it. Later my mom told me that she had spoken with them by phone and told them all about me. They would be my parents for the trip. They never once mentioned that I was going to be with my mother. That was by design because they knew that it would make me anxious and, also, maybe more difficult to handle.

So we went through Mexico. It was great because we stayed in hotels and I had good food to eat. I don't remember how long it took but we got to a house in Mexico and they left me with a strange woman. She was Mexican too. That was really scary because I didn't know her and I was confused. Where was my real mom? Why had I come on this journey? The house I stayed in was small and really hot. She kept the windows closed and my skin felt itchy. I remember having to wash with cold water. The lady was nice at first but I was there a long time. I got bored and restless. Later, my mom told me that the plan had been to bring me into the US through a regular border crossing. The smuggler paid an agent on the US side to let me in on a particular day. But apparently he didn't come to work on that day or for the two days after that. Meanwhile, as time went on the Mexican lady got really mean. She fed me quesadillas at every meal. When I refused to eat she screamed at me. I was so afraid. I couldn't sleep. I couldn't go outside. I felt trapped.

I didn't know until much later that the Mexican lady demanded $500 more to keep me the extra time and warned that if my mom didn't pay they would not be responsible for me. By the third day my mom was starting to panic. She called the coyota and they discussed a different plan. The coyota told her that there was a group waiting at the Rio Grande and they were planning to cross at 11:00 p.m. that night. Apparently in that group there was another woman with her nine-year-old daughter. The coyota told my mom that the best option was for me to cross with that group. One of the men in the group would carry me across the river on his shoulders. My mom knew that was much more dangerous but she felt that she had no choice. So she agreed.

The night we left they woke me up and took me to the river. I liked whispering with the other little girl. It was cooler outside and the night was dark. The man put me on his shoulders and started to wade into the water. I don't remember being afraid. Actually, I thought that it was kind of an adventure. The coyota called my mom a few hours before we went to the river and told her to pray because the whole area on the US side was crawling with immigration agents. My mom told me that she was so upset when she went to her night job at the Springfield shopping center that she couldn't do anything. Her coworkers covered for her. She called the coyota seven times and never got an answer. She was sure that the crossing had gone bad, that I had drowned or been caught by immigration and was in a cell somewhere.

Anyway we got to the other side and they put us on a bus. I remember it was like a big luxurious tour bus or maybe it just seemed like that because of the dingy house in Mexico. I remember arriving at that coyota's house in Houston. It was so big and beautiful with nice grounds around it. There was a bathroom with a big tub where I took a bath with bubbles and then went to sleep. I was finally comfortable. When I woke up the coyota called my mom and she promised that we would be together soon. I wanted to go inside that phone and hold her.

I begged my mom to come and get me herself but she couldn't. It was a long trip from Virginia to Texas and the coyota had it all arranged. Two men would drive me to Virginia. My mom wanted to know if the drivers were older men or young. She didn't like the fact that they were young. But when she questioned the plan, the coyota said, "I don't think that you want to risk having your daughter deported now that she has finally made it to the US." That really sounded like a threat so my mom agreed. They gave me a pill so that I would go to sleep on the ride. If people saw me with two young men, they would get suspicious.

I was so happy when we got to Virginia. They put me in the car with my mom and the man who was her boyfriend. I didn't want to wear a seat belt because I wanted to sit in her lap. She told me that I was in the US and we could call my grandma, my cousins, and the whole family and tell them that everything worked out. I was expecting a big beautiful house like the one I stayed in when we got to Houston. Instead, my mother was renting a small room in someone else's house that we had to share. I was so disappointed. Because we lived with other people, there were so many rules to follow. My mom tried to make it nice. She bought me a bed and Disney sheets. In the beginning I was happy and felt safe but then everything changed. Suddenly English was everywhere and I felt so lost.

My mom promised to buy a TV but I just got mad and said that I wanted to live somewhere else. I was unhappy and really afraid to start school. She told me that I would have to walk to school by myself. She promised that I would get used to it and I would learn to like it. I asked why we couldn't spend the day together? She was always working and I had to have a baby-sitter stay with me overnight because she worked from 6:00 p.m. to 5:00 a.m. I remember the first day of school. All the corridors in the school looked the same and I couldn't tell where I was. Everything was so different and at first, I hated it. For example, the school day in El Salvador was so much shorter. We were released at 1 p.m. for the day. I had gone to a private school there and I did take an English class but it didn't seem relevant. So I didn't learn anything.

2014

I started first grade in September and by March, I was getting used to it. One of the best things that year was meeting Marcia, the school counselor who worked with the Spanish kids. Whenever I had problems or was down, I went to see her. She was always there for me. I remember that by Christmas I could say a lot of English words. I started to memorize words and then I began to put them together. It was amazing the first time I read a short book in English by myself. I practiced saying the words out loud while I looked at myself in the mirror. I made a video of myself using the English names for my toys, clothes, shoes, and bed. I ended the video by telling the audience that I could speak English. I got good grades and by the end of the year, I had friends and the teacher named me a class leader. I had problems in math and I still do. It was confusing and seemed pointless to me. Whether it was unit volume or geometry or prealgebra or the surface area of something, I was more interested in reading books and learning to write.

My mom always pushed me to do well and to follow the rules. When I was in the second grade I got into trouble because I tried to steal my friend's flower. The school called my mom and she had to come to a meeting with the counselor and I. They told us that stealing is not allowed. When we got home my mom said that I was a guest in this country and what I did was a big deal. She said that stealing has consequences and the law has to be respected. She punished me by hitting me with a belt. I told my friend in school the next day and she said that kids here have rights and corporal punishment is against the law in this country. My friend said that I could have my mother arrested for beating me. I was angry with her at the time but now I know how high the stakes are for kids without papers.

I grew to love school and I know that I want to be a writer. I want to write fiction and I have all sorts of ideas for stories. One is about a girl who has the same nightmare every night. It is scary but creative. I have a cousin who drives me crazy because she is just wasting her life. She has no idea about what she wants to do and could care less about school. Last spring, she boasted on Snapchat and Instagram that she was failing all her classes. She eventually dropped out of high school. She is eighteen now and has nothing. Of course, she can mess up without any consequences because she is a US citizen. I am working really hard even though I am undocumented.

Teresa:

The man who took me to pick her up was my boyfriend. He was very different from the men I knew in El Salvador. He attended church services regularly and spent many hours volunteering there. He was respected and liked by everybody. But it had always been just Sonia and I when we lived in El Salvador. She was just six years old when she arrived in 2013 and she was so jealous of him. He would bring me flowers and chocolate. She would eat the chocolate and pour shampoo in the water to kill the flowers. If he took my hand, she would want me to hold hers instead. If he sat next to me she would push him away. It was so hard that I decided to end the relationship. But then, in 2014, I got pregnant with his child. It was a total shock because I had had my tubes tied before I left El Salvador. When Sonia found out she got so excited because she wanted a little brother or sister. Because of that pregnancy I married the father. Sonia loved the idea that we were husband and wife since she never really knew her father.

Sonia:

When I first arrived in the US, one of the big changes was getting used to my mother's boyfriend. I didn't want him around. I wanted her for myself. I hated it when he held her hand and when they slept in the same bedroom. When he bought her things, I threw them away or broke them. I am not sure that I ever really liked him but I liked the idea of having a father. I decided that I wanted her to buy me a sibling—everything else here is for sale. So when she got pregnant I was so excited. Of course, now that I have a little brother, I think that he is totally annoying. He wants everything I have. When she and her boyfriend decided to get married, at first I thought it was really cool. Plus he rented us our own apartment.

Teresa:

That's right. When she came, I was renting a room and after we got married he moved us into our own apartment. At first he was a good husband and treated us both well. He was proud to be a father and would buy things for the baby and take us out to eat. But after my baby boy was born he started to change. He would get angry for no reason and that would lead to insults or silences. He would boast about his money, that he had a second apartment, his own car, and wore nice clothes. He would stay with us at our apartment but then suddenly disappear for days at a time with no explanation. He wouldn't answer his phone. I tried not to get upset or to provoke him because that always led to fights. I did not want Sonia to see that. Despite our problems, he insisted that a civil ceremony didn't count and so we were married in the church.

2015

The fall that Sonia started third grade, I noticed that she was not eating when we were at the dinner table together. I was worried and asked her why. She would not talk about it and my husband scoffed at my concern saying that she was probably having problems in school. That didn't make sense to me. Sonia had started school two years before as a first grader and learned so quickly that by June she was named a class leader. Her teacher said that she was doing the same work as her American classmates. So if it wasn't her schoolwork, was she being bullied? Did someone taunt her about having no legal papers?

Marcia, the staff member who worked with Spanish-speaking parents at her school, had a special relationship with Sonia. When I first came here I didn't know how things worked and I was afraid to come out of the shadows. My friends told me not to enroll her in school. They said that I could get caught because I had been detained at the border and released with a notice to appear in immigration court. I passed my credible fear interview and was released but I never went to my court hearing in Texas. I had no family in Texas and no lawyer to help me so I came to Virginia. Marcia explained that all kids, regardless of their legal status, have a right to public education here. So Marcia helped me with the school paperwork.

Marcia noticed that Sonia was withdrawn and anxious so they had a talk. Sonia admitted that her stepfather had been going into her bedroom at night when I was at work and touching in her private places. He said that it was their special alone time so not to tell me. She didn't know what was happening until her third grade teacher taught a lesson on sexual abuse and explained what kind of behavior was not only inappropriate but against the law. Marcia called Child Protective Services and a social worker interviewed me and then reported the abuse to the Fairfax County police.

Sonia:

Things were good for a while but after my little brother was born things changed. My stepfather was spending less time at the apartment and although my mom tried to hide it I would heard them fighting. She was still working nights and he started to come into my bedroom. At first he got on the bed and just hugged me but then he began to touch me in my private places. I was afraid to fall asleep and when he opened the door to my room I could smell his aftershave before I could see him. I didn't understand what was happening but I knew that it wasn't right because he said not to tell anyone. It wasn't until I learned about the different forms of child abuse in school that I confided in Marcia.

2006

Teresa:

I was devastated to learn what was happening. The unbelievable part is that I had experienced the same thing in El Salvador. How could this happen again? When I was only fifteen, I was raped by a man who was twenty-six years older than me. I was in the seventh grade and he was the principal of my school. After the first time, he forced me to continue to have sex with him. I lived with my grandparents and I tried to tell my grandma what was happening. She accused me of lying because the principal had a great reputation in the town—just like my husband here in the US. When they saw that I already had a baby in the womb it was a bit late to question my word. I wanted them to call the police but my grandfather refused. No, he said, it would be better to make him support you. So my grandfather and the school principal agreed that he would pay for the delivery, a decent place for us to live, and private school fees. He did as he promised but as soon as I recovered from the cesarean section he expected the sex to continue. I felt trapped because my grandparents were poor and I had no other means of support. Some of my friends said don't rock the boat. He has money, several houses, and a car. Why not keep things the way they were? But they had no idea how bad it was or the kind of things he made me do. How could I trust him to be around a little girl? In my new school, I got a government scholarship that paid for tuition and gave me some independence. I had promised myself that I would protect Sonia from that kind of abuse and yet I was living with a man who had been fondling her on a regular basis.

2015

We went to the Fairfax family court and Child Protective Services interviewed me. They believed that I had no idea about the abuse and asked me to help the police with their investigation. They told me to pretend that nothing had happened so they could gather more evidence. I tried to hide it but it was unthinkable for me to be intimate with him. I couldn't help asking him if he had ever hurt a little girl or touched her sexually? He asked me why I was asking. But he began to suspect that I had gone to the police. Then he received a notice to report to the police station for questioning. He didn't go and instead withdrew all the money from our bank account. A friend told me that he was planning to leave the country so I called the police. They issued an all-points bulletin to the airlines and an employee at National airport saw the alert and he was arrested before he could get on the plane.

That was the beginning of a legal nightmare because the case had to go to court. I was a wreck, working two jobs, caring for my kids and dealing with the case. We had to leave the apartment my husband had rented and went back to paying for a single room in a house. Our guardian angel, Marcia, helped me find a good attorney. The case dragged on for two years with depositions and hearings. There was pressure from the members of our church who refused to believe that anything had happened. They insisted that my husband was a good man and had done so much

for the congregation. Others said, "Why not just forgive him and stay together?" I could never forget that he would have left the country with all
our money.

The lawyer asked Sonia to describe what happened and to write a letter
in English to the judge. She composed a very strong letter. The good news is
that my husband was convicted, sentenced to five years in prison, and then
deported. Even his family in Virginia admitted that he was sick and said to
please deport him. Afterward other young girls came forward to say that
he had also abused them.

Sonia:

When I confided in Marcia, that started a huge investigation with the police and child services. I think sometimes that I shouldn't have said anything
because afterward the situation just got worse. He got kicked out of the
country and for a while my mom didn't have a job. Plus we lost the apartment and we are back to renting a room.

2017

Teresa:

My cooperation with the police allowed me to earn a U visa. As an undocumented immigrant, that visa gave me legal protection because I helped US
law enforcement to bring a criminal to justice. After four years, I can apply
for a green card and then ultimately become an American citizen. I have
decided that I am finished with men. I never want another man near me
again. My children are my life and I will devote myself entirely to them.

The U nonimmigrant status (U visa) was created for undocumented
victims of certain crimes who have suffered mental or physical abuse
and who cooperate with law enforcement or government officials in the
investigation or prosecution of criminal activity. Congress created the U
visa with the passage of the Victims of Trafficking and Violence Protection Act in October 2000. The legislation was intended to strengthen
law enforcement agencies' ability to prosecute cases of domestic vio-

lence, sexual assault, trafficking of noncitizens, and other crimes, while also protecting victims who have suffered substantial mental or physical abuse because of the crime.[3]

Sonia:
But now things are okay and I am starting to write my own stories.

Marcia:
Teresa has moved heaven and earth to protect her daughter. They moved nine times in one year because of the stepdad. At one point, she was not working, and until she received the U visa, she was undocumented. With all the ICE raids in Fairfax County in 2017, it was hard to help her. But we managed to get a special bus arrangement for Sonia so she could stay in the same school. She is so motivated to learn English and to do well. By hook or by crook Teresa took charge and I know that these two will make it.

This story is a testament to resilience and strength in the face of overwhelming adversity in the home country and in the United States. Who among us could overcome domestic violence in two places, a life-threatening injury in Mexico, near death in the Sonoma desert, harsh conditions in prison, the uncertainty of work without papers, and the challenges of dealing with US law enforcement while raising two young children alone?

It is also a testament to the critical support provided to immigrant parents and children from the committed staff in the Fairfax County school system. Without their help, Teresa would not have found a competent pro bono attorney who could help her secure a U visa and help ensure that Sonia could stay in the school where she blossomed academically. This story is also a testament to the doors that open for young immigrants who learn the language, excel in school, find acceptance among their peers, and discover a skill that will serve them for the rest of their lives. It is a sure return on the investment in the human capital that immigrants represent.

Conclusion

US Immigration in the Twenty-First Century

The stories of these women raise important questions about the state of immigration to the United States in the twenty-first century. Overall, immigrants and their US-born children now make up over a quarter of the US population. The share of the foreign-born population has risen steadily since 1970 and the number of undocumented immigrants in the United States is currently estimated to be approximately 11 million. Roughly two-thirds of the undocumented population have lived in the United States for more than a decade, and many are the parents of US-born children. The women in this book fit this pattern. Out of the ten included, six came to the United States between 2000 and 2005 and have spent between sixteen and twenty-two years living, working, and paying taxes. All but two left their children behind with a mother or sibling when they headed north and the majority were separated from their children for years before being reunited in the United States. Since coming to the United States, some have found new partners and four have had children while living here. All but one fled extreme violence in their Northern Triangle countries. Their primary motivation in leaving home was to seek protection and a safe place in the United States.

Many years later, the dream of attaining legal status remains out of reach for all but one. Teresa qualified for a U visa and is on a pathway to citizenship only because her daughter was the victim of a serious crime in the United States. If Teresa and the mothers in this book had found competent legal representation and had known how to petition for asylum, they may well have been granted this form of relief. Given the significant increases in migrants seeking asylum from all over the world—including Colombia, Cuba, Haiti, and Venezuela—and the huge case backlogs in immigration courts, we should ask ourselves what can be done to better adjudicate claims for legal status. How can we ensure that the civil and human rights of migrants are not violated while their claims are processed? Currently, there are very few avenues for gaining legal status. Given the large number of undocumented immigrants who have lived and worked in the United States for years, how can they become permanent legal residents in the United States? What follows are some proposed solutions to address the crisis surrounding undocumented immigration.

Reform the Avenues for Legal Residence

US immigration law is based on a complicated set of principles that involve the reunification of families, the admittance of immigrants with skills that are valuable to the US economy, the protection of refugees, and the promotion of diversity. Because family reunification is a bedrock principle for legal entry, an unlimited number of visas are available every year for the immediate relatives of US citizens—"immediate relatives" only includes spouses of US citizens, unmarried children under twenty-one, and parents of US citizens. In order to be admitted through the family-based immigration system, a US citizen or Legal Permanent Resident sponsor must petition for an individual relative, establish the legitimacy of the relationship, meet minimum income requirements, and sign an affidavit of support stating that the sponsor will be financially responsible for the family members in the United States. The individual relative must also meet certain eligibility requirements that include submitting to a medical exam and obtaining required vaccinations (including for COVID-19), passing an analysis of any immigration or criminal history, and demonstrating that they will not become primarily dependent on the government for subsistence. All other family members are part of a family preference system in which there are annual caps on available visas and the wait for available visas can last for years.

In addition to the numerical limits placed on the various immigration preference categories, the Immigration and Nationality Act also places a limit on how many immigrants can come to the United States from any one country. Currently, no group of permanent immigrants (family-based and employment-based combined) from a single country can exceed 7 percent of the total number of people immigrating to the United States in a single fiscal year. One means to help mitigate the crisis surrounding undocumented immigration would be to provide additional green cards for members of the extended family who meet the government's requirements. The US government should also create seasonal visas in agriculture and construction to allow migrant workers to work temporarily and then return to their home country.[1]

Monitor Don't Detain Asylum seekers

In 2022, the Biden administration was finally able to end the Trump policy that forced thousands of asylum seekers to wait in dangerous areas in Mexico while their cases were pending.[2] During his presidential campaign, Biden had pledged to suspend the Remain in Mexico policy and end "for-profit" detention. He made good on the first promise but failed to deliver on the second. His January 26, 2021, executive order eliminated the use of private prisons and banned the renewal of contracts for privately operated Department of Justice (DOJ) prisons—which include Bureau of Prisons and US Marshals facilities. Unfortunately, the order failed to include privately run Immigration and Customs Enforcement (ICE) detention centers, which operate under the Department of Homeland Security (DHS). While private prisons make up less than 10 percent of the total US prison and jail system, 79 percent of people in immigration detention were held in private prisons as of September 2021.[3]

Rather than end immigration detention, the Biden administration expanded it, sometimes holding people in the same prisons that he had deemed too unsafe for criminals. Reports emerged that local governments and private prison corporations were in talks to convert

additional Department of Justice-contracted private prisons to ICE detention centers. In 2022 these efforts were already under way at facilities
including the West Tennessee Detention Facility, and the Leavenworth
Detention Facility in Kansas, where local governments were negotiating
agreements to convert the facilities into ICE detention centers.[4] In my
home state of Georgia, the private corrections company GEO Group
reached an agreement with Charlton County (near the Florida-Georgia
border) to nearly quadruple the number of beds for federal immigration detention from 780 to 3,018. If the government filled all the beds,
it would constitute one of the largest immigration detention complexes
in the nation.[5]

Immigration detention is one of the fastest growing and most profit-
able forms of mass incarceration in the nation. Detention centers are
intentionally located in remote areas where costs are cheap, good jobs
are scarce, and access to attorneys is very limited. It is well documented
that for-profit prisons put people's lives and health at great risk, violate
principles of human rights, and flout due process protections. The lack
of federal oversight means that medical neglect and physical abuse of the
detained largely go unchecked. Another means to help ameliorate the
current devastating circumstances surrounding undocumented immigration in the US would be for the federal government to fully phase out
the use of immigration detention, cancel contracts with ICE, and, most
importantly, redirect a portion of ICE's $6 billion dollar budget to fund
legal representation for asylum seekers in immigration court hearings.[6]
Recent data on migration shows that enforcement-based approaches do
not deter families who flee violence. Since 2014, the number of families
arriving at the southern border has continued to increase. During the
time of the family separation policy, between April and July 2018, family
arrivals remained constant at approximately nine thousand people per
month. Heightened enforcement at the border creates the conditions
in which smugglers and organized criminal groups can profit from the
need to overcome barriers to enter the United States, benefiting smugglers without deterring migration.[7]

Fix the Immigration Court System

Asylum seekers in the United States must navigate an immigration court system that a *Washington Post* editorial described as "a diorama of dysfunction" and "Dickensian impenetrability operating under comically antiquated conditions."[8] Operating with a small fraction of the budget allocated for enforcement agencies—just one-sixtieth—the immigration courts are plagued by staff shortages, huge backlogs, lengthy delays for cases to be heard, burnout of judges, and negative press. People in immigration court proceedings do not have the right to appointed counsel, even if they are under eighteen years of age. Given the complexity of US immigration law, it is impossible to successfully petition for asylum without legal representation. Yet, 40 percent of people cannot find lawyers to represent them, and almost all—approximately 85 percent—speak a language other than English, making their ability to represent themselves all but impossible. If they are fortunate enough to find a volunteer attorney with knowledge of immigration law, their effort to seek protection can become mired for years in a court backlog of four hundred thousand pending asylum cases.

Petitioners must make an asylum claim in a system where power imbalances threaten judicial independence, fairness, and due process. Immigration courts are part of the executive branch of government and are located within the DOJ, an agency whose primary mission is law enforcement. Immigration judges are expected to exercise independent judgment despite the fact that, like government prosecutors, they are employees of the DOJ and must rule on cases brought by that department.[9]

The operating procedures for immigration courts are written by political appointees, not by judges, and often favor the government. Because immigration judges work for the DOJ they have little control over their dockets or the time spent on individual cases. Some judges carry caseloads of five thousand cases or more, usually with limited support staff. To better distribute caseloads, reduce burnout, and ensure due process protections, the government needs to increase the number of judges as well as the number of lawyers and clerks. Administrators who have little or no experience as judges closely monitor dockets and pressure immigration judges to complete cases more quickly or risk unsatisfactory performance evaluations.[10] In contrast, the prosecutors who represent the government in court have virtually unfettered discretion to initiate removal proceedings, make release determinations, and control the information central to the case. However, they are protected from sanctions for unprofessional conduct.

The stakes in asylum hearings are so high because the benefits are life changing. The grant of asylum comes with work authorization, a social security number, eligibility for government assistance, the ability to petition for immediate family members, and a pathway to US citizenship. In contrast, a denial of asylum can amount to a death sentence when petitioners are deported to the situations of harm that they fled. The law gives individual judges the discretion to determine credibility in asylum cases, a situation that produces huge variations in grant rates and has been described as "refugee roulette." In contrast, judges have no discretion to allow someone to remain in the United States based solely on hardship or humanitarian reasons. In addition, the attorney general has the power to overturn settled case law on asylum, injecting political considerations into judicial decisions that should have no place in an independent court. Moving the immigration courts out of the executive branch of government would be an important step in making transparency and public access paramount and in allowing judicial proceedings to be handled by independent adjudicators.

Streamline the Asylum Process

The Biden administration proposed a significant overhaul to the system for screening migrants for asylum eligibility at the southern border. What they describe as the "asylum officer rule" would rely more on the corps of asylum officers rather than immigration judges to determine who gets legal relief. Because of current case backlogs and the shortage of judges, asylum hearings are now scheduled years in the future. Biden officials described this new policy as their most significant border policy initiative and aimed for it to streamline an overburdened court system by processing more cases faster. DHS secretary Alejandro Mayorkas said in a statement, "Individuals who qualify for asylum will receive protection more swiftly, and those who are not eligible will be promptly removed rather than remaining in the U.S. for years while their cases are pending. We are delivering justice quickly, while also ensuring due process."[11] Although the new policy was immediately challenged in a lawsuit by Texas attorney general Ken Paxton (R), it would be an important first step in alleviating the current gridlock in immigration courts that can trap asylum seekers in longer and longer periods of legal limbo.[12]

The rules governing asylum decisions reflect Cold War realities. Since 1965 when the Immigration and Nationality Act revamped the immigration system, definitions of persecution have favored those fleeing communist or communist-dominated nation states. In contrast, those fleeing right-wing dictatorships who supported US policies have often failed to win refugee status. A case in point is the Haitian regime run by the Duvalier family from 1957 to 1986. The Duvaliers supported American foreign policy in the Western Hemisphere and the Cold War. Because of this, the US State Department turned a blind eye to horrific state-sponsored violence and repression and granted few Haitians refugee status. The definitions for persecution should recognize nonstate actors such as criminal gangs and cartels that operate with impunity or with the collusion of governments in Central and South America.

Given the dire situations faced by those fleeing violence and abuse in their home countries, we should stop playing politics with the number of refugees admitted annually to the United States. Each year, the president consults with Congress to determine the numerical ceiling for refugee admissions. The overall cap imposes limits for each region of the world. After September 11, 2001, the number of refugees admitted into the United States fell drastically. When the Bush administration put new security checks in place, annual refugee admissions returned to their previous levels and rose during the Obama administration. During the Trump administration, the refugee ceiling fell sharply and in fiscal year (FY) 2020, the ceiling was set at an all-time low of 18,000. In that year, the lowest number of refugees were admitted since the creation of the system in 1980—only 11,817.[13] The FY 2021 ceiling was set at 15,000 refugees by the Trump administration but was subsequently raised to 62,500 in 2021 and again in FY 2022 to 125,000 by the Biden administration. However, by nearly the end of FY 2022 only 7,637 refugees had been admitted.

Protect DACA—Better Yet, Pass the Dream Act

As the Deferred Action for Childhood Arrivals (DACA) program turned ten in 2022, the legality of the program was challenged in court by a federal lawsuit filed by Republican officials in Texas and several other states. Created as an executive order during the Obama administration, the DACA program gives undocumented youth who came as children to the United States a reprieve from deportation and temporary legal status. By 2022 the program had offered about 825,000 young people a chance to change their lives if they met eligibility requirements that allowed them to apply for renewable two-year work permits, Social Security cards, and driver's licenses.

As important as DACA is for the young people who qualify, it remains a stopgap measure that can be terminated by any occupant of the Oval Office. The Trump administration attempted to do just that, but the Supreme Court blocked its effort on a technicality. DACA would never have been necessary if Congress had passed the Dream (the Development, Relief, and Education for Alien Minors) Act. This legislation would give permanent legal status to young people who grew up in the Unites States and are American in every respect except for their legal status. It would have significant economic, political, and social benefits for the entire country.

The first version of the Dream Act was introduced in 2001. Since then, at least eleven versions of the Dream Act have been introduced in Congress, most often by Senator Dick Durban from Illinois. While there are different versions of the bill, they would all provide a pathway to legal status for undocumented people who came to this country as children. Some versions have garnered as many as 48 cosponsors in the US Senate and 152 in the House of Representatives. Despite bipartisan support for each bill, none have become law. To date, the 2010 bill came closest to full passage when it passed the House but fell just five votes short of the sixty needed to proceed in the Senate.

The most recent versions of the Dream Act would provide current, former, and future undocumented high school graduates and GED recipients a pathway to US citizenship through college, work, or the armed services. Depending on the eligibility requirements, it is estimated that roughly two to three million young people would benefit from this proposed legislation.[14] The Dream Act should be passed. We cannot in good conscience continue to marginalize so many young people with a stake in the future of this country when permanent protection would provide them with the same opportunities as their US-citizen peers.

Punish Misconduct by Customs and Border Protection Agents

The conduct of Customs and Border Protection (CBP) agents is important to examine since they are the first face of the United States that many migrants encounter when they attempt to enter the United States. Repeated reports reveal a culture of racism that has persisted in the US Border Patrol throughout the agency's history. Over the past century, Border Patrol agents have perpetrated violence on migrants "in the form of killing, sexual assault, excessive force, and verbal degradation—all with impunity."[15] In the wake of explosive reports by ProPublica of violent, racist, and sexist postings in private CBP Facebook groups online, the House Oversight and Reform Committee began an investigation in 2019. Committee investigators tried for more than a year to obtain access to witnesses and unredacted disciplinary records, but the Trump administration refused to comply, even when presented with a subpoena.

In February 2021 the Biden administration finally gained access to the records. The House report that was made public in October 2021 revealed that CBP's Discipline Review Board recommended firing as many as twenty-four agents for "serious misconduct." Two retired but the rest received "significantly lighter" punishments instead. According to the report, only eighteen of the twenty-four were suspended, another got a reprimand letter, and still another an "oral admonishment." One of the two fired Border Patrol agents had posted offensive images of a "white supremacist symbol and sexualized images of a Member of Congress." The second dismissed agent shared "multiple offensive and abhorrent posts, including a doctored picture of a Member of Congress being violently sexually abused and raped," along with graphics and comments bullying subordinates.

Of the sixty agents who committed misconduct, the report found, fifty-seven of them continue to work with migrants today. "The vast majority of agents—including those who made degrading and even threatening comments about migrants—received only minor discipline," the report said. The Department of Homeland Security, including CBP, initiated an internal review in 2021 directed by Secretary Alejandro Mayorkas "to identify and terminate intolerable prejudice, and to reform policies and training." The report recommends that CBP leaders hold social media violators accountable. They should reform hiring processes to screen out applicants with "records of discrimination" and consider such violations when deciding future promotions. It also indicates that officials should prevent employees who display bias from working with "vulnerable" populations such as children and address poor morale.[16] These are all measures that ought to be enacted.

Stop the War Against Migrants

Since Trump launched his presidential campaign in 2015 by labeling undocumented migrants as rapists and criminals and then depicted all unaccompanied minors in his 2018 State of the Union address as murderous predators, anti-immigrant rhetoric has become an effective political weapon. The power of incendiary media demonizing migrants can lead directly or indirectly to violence against them. The violence generated by the media stretches in a long line from the dehumanizing treatment of detained migrants by the former Arizona sheriff of Maricopa County, Joe Arpaio, and the punitive separation of parents and children in 2018, to the 2019 mass shooting by a white supremacist at a Walmart in El Paso, Texas, which left twenty-three people dead, the majority of them Latino. The Texas governor, Greg Abbott, acknowledged the role his rhetoric may have played in pushing the shooter to action. He had warned of a plot to transform his home state of Texas through illegal immigration. Just three years later, in a tightening reelection campaign with Democratic challenger Beto O'Rouke, he used the same tactic. He spoke openly of an invasion underway at the southern border, a move that would enable Texas to claim war powers and usurp the federal government's authority. Under Abbott's policies, Texas has spent approximately $4 billion on border security including detaining thousands of immigrants in state facilities on misdemeanor trespassing charges, deploying thousands of National Guard troops to the border, building more than twenty miles of new border wall, and paying to bus some immigrants to Washington, DC, and New York City. He also reinforced security in Texas border towns, although little serious crime is attributed to border crossers. In April of 2022, he played havoc with cross-border commerce by ordering safety inspections on trucks entering Texas from Mexico—a policy that produced no significant seizures of narcotics, guns, or other contraband.[17]

Despite the anti-immigrant rhetoric, numerous polls reveal that large majorities of Americans consider immigration a good thing, although they remain wary of the threats posed by illegal immigration. Similarly, a poll conducted by Vox and Data in 2020 found that 69 percent of voters—including a majority of Republicans—supported a pathway to citizenship for the undocumented if they meet certain requirements.[18] At a time when the United States is experiencing a demographic shortfall and high daily retirements, we need more low and high skill immigrant workers and new channels to permit them to enter and remain legally in the United States.[19]

This book concludes by reminding us of a quote from Luna, the Honduran mother who has lived and worked without legal status in this country for thirteen years. It is a plea to make good on the promise that the United States symbolizes for immigrants like her:

> When I crossed, I was not apprehended so they have no record of me. I know that I am not eligible for papers but, more than anything, I want my children to be legal. My Latina neighbors really discouraged me from going to immigration court for my kids because they said that we would just get detained and kicked out. I said that I have to follow the rules and obey the law to protect them. I left Honduras to save myself and to give my children a better life. I knew that I couldn't go to the police about the abuse. There was a Commission on Human Rights in Honduras but it didn't protect women like me. That kind of behavior is just normal for men. I was blind then. I only had my eyes opened once I got here. I know now that I have rights and can use them.

ACKNOWLEDGMENTS

I want to begin by thanking the artist Carolina Corona for drawing the powerful picture on the cover of the book. She drew the picture in just a few hours after hearing some of the stories of the migrant mothers who were seeking asylum in the US after being apprehended and detained in the immigration prison in Dilley, Texas in 2018. I am grateful to the immigration attorneys who first alerted the wider advocacy community to the injustices of a detention system that targets young migrant families seeking protection in the United States. At a 2017 conference at the University of the District of Columbia Law School, immigration attorneys Katy Murdza and Bridget Cambria made a moving appeal for volunteers to help screen asylum seekers who were detained for long periods in appalling conditions in ICE prisons in Texas and Pennsylvania. We all owe a debt of gratitude to the CARA pro bono attorneys and staff in the immigration prisons in Dilley and Karnes City, Texas, who worked tirelessly to help detained mothers clear the first hurdle in their quest for asylum. I joined the hundreds of women and men who traveled to Texas from all over the United States to volunteer in 2017 and 2018. We were inspired by lead attorney Shalyn Fluarty's leadership of the CARA project and the expert guidance she provided to all the volunteers. That experience made a lasting impression on me both because of the courage displayed by the mothers we interviewed and because of the violence they had suffered at home, on the journey, and, too often, at the hands of American immigration authorities.

In 2017, I volunteered in both ICE prisons in Texas with Debbie Boehm. She is an exemplary colleague, trusted friend, and one of the most prominent immigration scholars in the United States. We were collaborators on a number of research projects and also co-edited a volume on immigrant youth that was published in 2019, *Illegal Encounters: The Effect of Detention and Deportation on Young People.* I returned to volunteer at the prison in Dilley, Texas, in 2018 with a Cuban-American friend, Diane Lanevi. Her family fled political persecution in Cuba after Castro's rise to power and settled in Miami. Spending twelve-hour days interviewing detained mothers was one of the most intense and heartbreaking experiences I have ever had. It would not have been bearable without the support of those two women.

After I moved to Savannah, I met an Episcopal priest, Reverend Leeann Culbreath, who has been a vocal opponent of immigration detention since 2016. She has advocated for the women and men detained in ICE facilities in Georgia, particularly at the Irwin County Detention Center in Ocilla. In order to provide moral support for those in detention, she organized and trained volunteers to do prison visitations. In 2019, I took a group of volunteers to visit detained women in Irwin Detention Center. Leeann provided a wonderful orientation for us and arranged a meeting with the attorneys who provide free legal counsel to detainees. Leeann has been an outspoken critic of the pervasive medical abuse, neglect, and appalling living conditions at all the ICE prisons in Georgia. She and other advocates were instrumental in helping close Irwin Detention Center after credible reports surfaced of migrant women being sterilized without their knowledge or consent. In early 2020, Leeann Culbreath traveled to Savannah to join a panel discussion with Debbie Boehm and I in conjunction with the publication of *Illegal Encounters.*

My heartfelt thanks go to Robin Hamby, the founder and former director of the Immigrant Family Reunification and Parent Liaison program in the public schools in Fairfax County, Virginia. Robin allowed me to attend the September 2017 meeting with her entire staff and to meet the women who enroll immigrant youth in school, teach classes for immigrant parents, and serve as liaisons between the families, the children, and the school. Robin also encouraged me to observe the family reunification and Parent Project classes that were offered for immigrant parents who had recently been reunited with their children in the United States. I owe special thanks to instructors Mary Specht and Claudia Thomas, who taught the classes that I observed in 2017 and 2018 and to Marcia St John-Cunning who provided a critical lifeline to the Salvadoran mother and daughter I respectively call Teresa and Sonia in the book. I am also deeply indebted to Robin for connecting me with her program assistant, Ligia Diaz, who is a gifted researcher in her own right. She was an invaluable guide for me because of the caring relationships she had cultivated with immigrant families in the Fairfax schools. This book would not have been possible without her assistance in introducing me to mothers who agreed to tell their stories. Ligia was my research assistant throughout the 2017–18 academic year and accompanied me on all the interviews. The conversations that we had before and after the interviews helped shape my understanding of the women's lives in the home country and after their arrival in the United States.

As always, I am grateful for support from Georgetown University in the form of Graduate School Summer Research Fellowships in 2017 and 2018 and a Retired Faculty Research Grant in 2021. Funds from a presidential Reflective Engagement Grant awarded in 2014 made it possible for me to hire both Ligia Diaz and Eliana Lanfranco, then an undergraduate at Georgetown University, as my research assistants.

I had the good fortune to be named a Visiting Scholar at the School of Social Policy, Social Work, and Social Justice at the University College of Dublin in September and October of 2021. My thanks go to the Head of School and Professor of Social Work, James Campbell, for his enthusiastic welcome to the faculty and the university. My former colleague at Georgetown University, Ernesto Vasquez Del Aguila, now on the faculty at University College of Dublin, enthusiastically recommended me for the position. I am deeply indebted to Ernesto who was a wonderful interlocutor for my work and a terrific guide to Ireland's many sites. I enjoyed having the opportunity to write in lovely surroundings, get to know Dublin, explore the beautiful countryside outside the city, and meet so many warm and charming Irish people.

Some colleagues and friends have read portions of my work and given me invaluable feedback: Andy Bickford, Debbie Boehm, Leeann Culbreath, Diane Lanevi, Karen Moody, Susan Ossman, Roger Smith, Patti Sunderland, Susan Tauster, Ernesto Vasquez, and my husband, Steve. I also appreciate the thought-provoking questions I got following lectures that I gave in Dublin and in Savannah in 2019, 2020, and 2022. I am most grateful to the anonymous readers for New York University Press for their helpful comments on the manuscript.

Finally, my deepest gratitude goes to the mothers who agreed to share their stories with me and to invite their children into the conversation. All but one of them was undocumented but they welcomed me into their homes despite facing enhanced immigration enforcement that sent shock waves of fear throughout the local immigrant community in 2017–18. The testimonials they provide in this book invite us into their families, communities, and histories.

NOTES

INTRODUCTION

1 United Nations High Commissioner on Refugees, "Women on the Run," 4.
2 Frelick, Kysel, and Podkul, "Externalization of Migration," 191–92.
3 Benner and Jordan, "U.S. Ends Trump Policy."
4 Chisti and Bolter, "Biden at the One-Year Mark."
5 However, in the last three months of 2021, only 3,268 refugees resettled.
6 Barnes, "Supreme Court."
7 Editorial Board, "Deportation Policy."
8 US Customs and Border Protection, "Operational Update."
9 Terrio, *Whose Child*; Boehm and Terrio, *Illegal Encounters*.
10 Blitzer, "Private Detention Facility."
11 I partnered with a Nicaraguan woman, Ligia Penske Diaz, who was the assistant director of the program. She connected me with migrant mothers and accompanied me on interviews.

1. LUNA'S STORY

1 Kinskey, "Harsh Realities."
2 De Hoyos, Bussolo, and Núñez, "Maquila Booms."
3 United Nations High Commissioner for Human Rights, "Women on the Run," 23.
4 Hermannsdorfer, "Declaration," 11.
5 O'Donnell, "Quality of Democracy," 38–39.
6 Nazario, "Kill You," 7.
7 Freedom House, "Honduras."
8 Bauer et al., "Barriers to Health Care."
9 United Nations High Commissioner for Human Rights, "Women on the Run," 16.
10 Inter-American Commission on Human Rights, "Strategic Plan."
11 United States Department of State, "Human Rights."
12 Nazario, "Kill You," 6.
13 Ibid.
14 Sullivan, "Denied Asylum."
15 Palmer and Semple, "Portrait of Corruption."
16 United States Citizenship and Immigration Services, "Immigrant Services."
17 Ninety-two percent of Honduran children who applied for green cards through the SIJS visa on or after May 2016 were in deportation proceedings in

immigration courts compared to 27 percent of SIJS applicants from other countries. Aguilera, "Years Long Backlog."
18 Zawodny, "Immigration Court Backlog."
19 See the discussion of new protections provided to SIJS applicants by the Biden Administration in chapter 2.
20 Armstrong and Carlson, "Researching Guns."
21 Erez, Adelman, and Gregory, "Immigration and Domestic Violence," 51–52.

2. INES' STORY

1 Walsh and Menjívar, "Impunity," 589.
2 Sorensen, Tarzikan, and Heim, "El Salvador's Abortion Ban."
3 At this point in the narrative, Ines began to refer to the father of her children as her "husband." They never married, but he recognized all three of the children as his.
4 Walsh and Menjívar, "Impunity," 593.
5 United States Department of State, "El Salvador 2014."
6 Migrants from the south refer to the Rio Grande as the Rio Bravo.
7 Ayuda, located in Washington, DC, is an NGO that provides a wide range of immigration legal services to low-income immigrants in the greater DC area, including direct representation and the necessary guidance to navigate the complex immigration system. See https://www.ayuda.com.
8 Zawodny, "Immigration Court Backlog."
9 Davidson and Hlass, "They Can Deport Me," 35–36.
10 Sessions, "Zero-Tolerance Memorandum."
11 Shear et al., "Take Away the Children."
12 Matter of A-B. 27 I & N Dec. 316 (A.G. 2018).
13 Center for Gender and Refugee Studies, "Garland's Decision."
14 Musallo and Rice, "One Year Bar."
15 TRAC Immigration, "Asylum Success Varies."
16 TRAC Immigration, "Judge-by-Judge Asylum Decisions."
17 Borotto, "New Biden Administration."

3. SANDRA'S STORY

1 Kerwin et al., "U.S. Foreign-Born Essential Workers," 2.
2 According to estimates by the Salvadoran Central Reserve Bank, by 2015, there were roughly sixty thousand gang members in the country, and 70 percent of the country's businesses were being extorted, producing annual losses of $4 billion. Blitzer, "Strongman of the People."
3 On June 27, 2022, the bodies of forty-six migrants were found in the back of a sweltering tractor-trailer in San Antonio. San Antonio fire chief Charles Hood told reporters that there were no signs of water or working air conditioning in the truck. The bodies were hot to the touch when they were removed. Rescuers pulled

sixteen people from the truck who were still alive and conscious, including four minors. Although it is the deadliest smuggling incident of its kind in US history, it was only the latest in a long series of migrant deaths. Hernández, Miroff, and Sacchetti, "46 Migrants." This could have been the fate of Luis had the trip been longer or the weather hotter.

4 See the explanation for the SIJS visa in the chapters devoted to Luna's and Ines's stories.
5 Olivo, "Tensions over Immigration."
6 Lind, "Immigrants Coming to Kill You."
7 Trump, "Address to the Nation."
8 Sheila Gotti, interview with author, April 16, 2018, Twain Middle School, Fairfax County, Virginia.

4. ISABEL'S STORY

1 They had been granted Temporary Protected Status after the series of earthquakes struck El Salvador in 2001. This allowed them to work legally and travel freely between the United States and El Salvador.
2 Gilardi, "Ally or Exploiter."
3 On coyotes, see Sanchez and Zhang, "Rumors," 136–38.
4 González, "Navigating with Coyotes," 182, 187.
5 Vogt, "Stuck in the Middle," 367–68.
6 Slack and Campbell, "On Narco-coyotaje," 16.
7 Sanchez and Zhang, "Rumors," 145.
8 Ibid., 146.
9 Congressional Research Report, "El Salvador," 5–6.
10 Manning, "Ending Artesia."
11 Harlan, "Inside the Administration's 1 billion Deal"; Lowenstein, "Private Prisons."
12 Cantor and Johnson, "Detained, Deceived and Deported."
13 Eagley, Shafer, and Whally, "Detaining Families," 790–91.
14 Murphey, "Moving Beyond Trauma."
15 American Psychiatric Association, "ODD."
16 Yarris, *Care Across Generations*, 35.
17 Susie Stratham, interview with author, October 27, 2017, Mount Vernon High School, Fairfax County, Virginia.

5. MARIA'S STORY

1 Vogt, *Lives in Transit*.
2 Sanchez and Zhang, "Rumors," 137.
3 On September 14, 2020, in *Ramos v. Wolf*, the US Court of Appeals for the Ninth Circuit prohibited the Department of Homeland Security from terminating Temporary Protected Status for El Salvador, Haiti, Nicaragua, and Sudan.
4 Valdes, "Lawsuit."

6. NOHELY'S STORY

1 Vogt, "Stuck in the Middle," 373.
2 Dominguez-Villegas, "Strengthening Mexico's Protection," 5–6.
3 Ibid, 16.
4 Ibid, 15.
5 Human Rights Clinic at the University of Texas School of Law, "Control."
6 Martinez, Slack, and Heyman, *Bordering on Criminal*.
7 MSNBC, "Former Border Patrol Agent."
8 Dickinson, "'Guats,' 'Tonks,' and 'Subhuman Shit.'"
9 Ewing, "Legacy of Racism."
10 Women's Refugee Commission, "Forced from Home."
11 American Civil Liberties Union, "ACLU Obtains Documents."

7. ELISA'S STORY

1 Terrio, *Whose Child*, 136–38.
2 Gelatt, "Explainer."

8. THE PARENTING CLASSES

1 Fairfax County Public Schools, "About Us," accessed September 8, 2018, https://www.fcps.edu.
2 Robin Hamby introduced me to the class instructors and allowed me to attend the family reunification and parent project classes in 2017–18.
3 Tannen, *Talking 9 to 5*.
4 Class participants are led through a multistep process where they acknowledge blame and promise to never repeat the harm. They take turns practicing an apology with partners.
5 Mary Specht and Claudia Thomas are two of the instructors whose classes I regularly observed.
6 Paulina Hidalgo, interview with author, October 5, 2017, Herndon Middle School, Fairfax County, Virginia.
7 Susie Stratham, interview with author, October 27, 2017, Mount Vernon High School, Fairfax County, Virginia.
8 My undergraduate research assistant, Eliana Lanfranco, attended the classes with me in 2017.
9 Mam is a Mayan language spoken by approximately six hundred thousand people in the Guatemalan departments of Quetzaltenango, Huehuetenango, San Marcos, and Realhuleu as well as in the Mexican state of Chiapas.
10 Fry, Morgan, and Melendez, *Cómo cambiar la conducta destructiva*, 30.
11 Ibid., 96.
12 Nation Swell, "When Immigrant Families Struggle with Reunions, This Educator Can Help," accessed July 10, 2022, https://nationswell.com.

9. ROSALÍA'S STORY

1 Indigenous people are marginalized and subjected to discrimination based on their ethnicity compared to mestizos and whites.
2 Human Rights Watch, "Guatemala Events."
3 Avalo Tizol, *Indigenous Women's Bodies*, 5.
4 A Life and Family Protection bill that would expand the criminalization of abortion and raise the maximum prison sentence from three to ten years was under consideration by the Guatemalan Congress in 2021. Human Rights Watch, "Guatemala Events."
5 Singh, Prada, and Kestler, "Induced Abortion and Unintended Pregnancy," 136.
6 Ewing, "Legacy of Racism."
7 Menjívar, *Enduring Violence*, 66.
8 Chomat et al., "Maternal Health," 114.
9 Menjívar, *Enduring Violence*, 100.
10 Kids in Need of Defense, "Sexual and Gender-Based Violence."
11 Glenn-Levin Rodriguez, *Fragile Families*, 56–58.
12 Anonymous, interview with author, September 27, 2017.

10. VANIA'S STORY

1 This is a small town outside Ciudad Barrios in the department of San Miguel.
2 Congressional Research Report, "El Salvador," 5–6.
3 Human Rights Watch, "El Salvador Events."
4 Ibid.
5 Ibid.
6 Congressional Research Service, "El Salvador," 12.
7 Yarris, *Care Across Generations*.
8 Altar, a border town matching this description had become the epicenter of undocumented migration through the Sonoran desert by the mid-2000s when Vania crossed into the United States. Slack, *Deported to Death*, 40–41.
9 Menjívar, "Family Reorganization," 234–35.
10 Villaviciencio, "Waking Up," 31.

11. TERESA'S STORY

1 Slack, *Deported to Death*, 18–19.
2 Gilman, "The U.S. Deportation System."
3 United States Citizenship and Immigration Services, "Humanitarian Petitions."

CONCLUSION

1 American Immigration Council, "Fact Sheet."
2 Barnes, "Supreme Court."
3 Detention Watch Network, "Expanding Private Immigration Detention."

4 Ibid.
5 Redmon and Grinspan, "Exclusive: Ga. Immigration Facility."
6 Sacchetti, "ICE Holds Growing Numbers."
7 Roberts et al., "Migrant Smuggling Costs."
8 Editorial Board, "America's Immigration Courts."
9 Slavin and Mark, "You Be the Judge," 91–92.
10 Marks, "I'm an Immigration Judge."
11 Miroff, "Biden Prepares Asylum Overhaul."
12 The Texas lawsuit was heard by US District Court judge Matthew Kacsmaryk, an appointee of former president Donald Trump, who ruled against the Biden administration last year when he ordered the reinstatement of the "Remain in Mexico" policy. That case is now pending before the Supreme Court.
13 United States Department of State, "Proposed Refugee Admissions."
14 American Immigration Council, "Dream Act."
15 Ewing, "Legacy of Racism."
16 Sacchetti and Miroff, "Border Patrol Agents."
17 Editorial Board, "A Deportation Policy in Chaos."
18 Narea, "Poll."
19 Klobucista, Cheatham, and Roy, "The U.S. Immigration Debate."

BIBLIOGRAPHY

Aguilera, Jasmine. "A Years-Long Immigration Backlog Puts Thousands of Abused Kids in Limbo." *Time*, December 16, 2021. https://time.com/6128025.

American Academy of Child and Adolescent Psychiatry. "ODD: A Guide for Families." *Diagnostic Statistical Manual of Mental Disorders*. 5th ed. American Academy of Child and Adolescent Psychiatry, 2009.

American Civil Liberties Union. "ACLU Obtains Documents Showing Widespread Abuse of Child Immigrants in U.S. Custody." May 22, 2018. www.aclu.org.

American Immigration Council. "U.S. Customs and Border Protections' Systematic Denial of Entry to Asylum Seekers at Ports of Entry at the U.S.-Mexico Border." With the American Civil Liberties Association, American Immigration Lawyer's Association, Women's Refugee Commission, Kino Border Initiative, Texas Rio Grande Legal Aid, Inc, Latin America Working Group, Public Counsel. January 13, 2017. www.americanimmigrationcouncil.org.

———. "The Dream Act: An Overview." March 16, 2021. www.americanimmigration-council.org.

———. "Fact Sheet: How the United States Immigration System Works." September 14, 2021. www.americanimmigrationcouncil.org.

Armstrong, Madison, and Jennifer Carlson. "We've Spent Over a Decade Research-ing Guns in America. This Is What We Learned." *New York Times*, March 26, 2021. https://nytimes.com.

Avalos Tizol, Ana Gabriela. *Indigenous Women's Bodies: Primer Territorio de Defensa*. Master's thesis, University of San Francisco, 2019. https://repository.usfca.edu./thes/1189.

Barnes, Robert. "Supreme Court Clears Biden Administration to End Trump's 'Remain in Mexico' Policy." *Washington Post*, June 30, 2022. https://washingtonpost.com.

Barrick, Leigh. "Divided by Detention: Asylum-Seeking Families' Experience of Sepa-ration." *American Immigration Council*, August 31, 2016. https://www.americanim-migrationcouncil.org.

Bauer, Heidi M., Michael Rodriguez, Seline Szkupinski Quiroga, and Yvette G. Flores-Ortiz. "Barriers to Health Care for Abused Latina and Asian Immigrant Women." *Journal of Health Care for the Poor and Underserved* 11, no. 1 (2000): 33–44. https://doi:10.1353/hpu.2010.0590.

Benner, Katy, and Miriam Jordan. "U.S. Ends Trump Policy Limiting Asylum for Gang and Domestic Violence Survivors." *New York Times*, June 16, 2021. https://nytimes.com.

Blitzer, Jonathan. "The Private Georgia Immigration Detention Facility at the Center of a Whistle-Blower's Complaint." *New Yorker*, September 20, 2020. https://newyorker.com.

———. "Strongman of the People. How President Nayib Bukele Rode an Authoritarian Crackdown to Become Latin America's Most Popular Leader." *New Yorker*, September 12, 2022. https://newyorker.com.

Boehm, Deborah A. *Intimate Migrations: Gender, Family, and Illegality among Transnational Mexicans.* New York: New York University Press, 2012.

———. *Returned: Going and Coming in an Age of Deportation.* Oakland: University of California Press, 2016.

Boehm, Deborah A., and Susan J. Terrio, eds. *Illegal Encounters: The Effect of Detention and Deportation on Young People.* New York: New York University Press, 2019.

Borotto, Gianna. "New Biden Administration Policies Provide Crucial Protections for Immigration Youth." March 18, 2022. https://immigrationimpact.com.

Cantor, Guillaume, and Toby Johnson. "Detained, Deceived and Deported: Experiences of Recently Deported Central American Families." *American Immigration Council*, May 18, 2016. https://www.americanimmigrationcouncil.org.

CARA Family Pro Bono Project. "Update on recent ICE Enforcement Actions Targeting Central American Families." Accessed April 18, 2017.

Castillo-Granados, Dalie, and Yasmin Yavar. "A New Legal Framework for Children Seeking Special Immigrant Juvenile Status." *Richmond Public Interest Law Review* 20, no. 1 (2017): 49–61.

Center for Gender and Refugee Studies. "Attorney General Garland's Decision on Matter of A-B- and L-E-A Will Save Lives." June 16, 2021. https://cgrs.uchastings.edu.

Chisti, Muzaffar, and Jessica Bolter. "Biden at the One-Year Mark: A Greater Change in Direction on Immigration Than Is Recognized." *Migration Policy Institute*, January 19, 2022. https://www.migrationpolicy.org.

———. "Court-Ordered Relaunch of Remain in Mexico Policy Tweaks Predecessor Program, but Faces Similar Challenges." *Migration Policy Institute*, December 2, 2021. https://www.migrationpolicy.org.

Chomat, Anne Marie, Noel Solomon, Gabriela Montenegro-Bethancourt, and Caitlin Crowley. "Maternal Health and Health Seeking Behaviors among Indigenous Mam Mothers from Quetzaltenango, Guatemala." *Revista Panamaricana de Salud Pública* 35, no. 2 (2014): 113–20.

Coutin, Susan Bibler. *Exiled Home: Salvadoran Transnational Youth in the Aftermath of Violence.* Durham, NC: Duke University Press, 2016.

Davidson, Rachel Leya, and Laila L. Hlass. "'Any Day They Can Deport Me': Over 44,000 Immigrant Children Trapped in the SIJS Backlog." *End SIJS Backlog Coalition* and *Door*, November 2021. https://sijsbacklog.com.

Detention Watch Network, "The Biden Administration is Expanding Private Immigration Detention." September 29, 2021. www.detentionwatchnetwork.org.

De Hoyos, Rafael E., Maurizio Bussolo, Oscar Núñez. "Can Maquila Booms Reduce Poverty? Evidence from Honduras." Policy Research Working Paper 4789. Washington, DC: *World Bank*, 2008.

Diaz Prieto, Gabriela, and Gretchen Kuhner. *Women Fleeing Violence in Central America: Research Contributions for Understanding the Refugee Crisis*. Mexico City: The Institute of Women in Migration, 2016. https://imumi.org.

Dickinson, Tim. "'Guats,' 'Tonks,' and 'Subhuman Shit': The Shocking Texts of a Border Patrol Agent." *Rolling Stone*, June 13, 2019. www.rollingstone.com.

Dominguez-Villegas, Rodrigo. "Strengthening Mexico's Protection of Central American Unaccompanied Minors in Transit." *Migration Policy Institute*, July 2017. www.migrationpolicy.org.

Dreby, Joanna. *Everyday Illegal: When Policies Undermine Immigrant Families*. Oakland: University of California Press, 2015.

Eagley, Ingrid, Steve Shafer, and Jana Whally. "Detaining Families: A Study of Asylum Adjudication in Family Detention." *California Law Review* 106 (2018): 785–868.

Editorial Board. "America's Immigration Courts Are a Diorama of Dysfunction." *Washington Post*, January 9, 2017. www.washingtonpost.com.

———. "A Deportation Policy in Chaos—Thanks to One Judge." *Washington Post*, July 14, 2022. www.washingtonpost.com.

———. "In a Close Race Texas's Abbott Talks War—Against Migrants." *Washington Post*, July 15, 2022. www.washingtonpost.com.

Erez, Edna, Madelaine Adelman, and Carol Gregory. "Intersections of Immigration and Domestic Violence: Voices of Battered Immigrant Women." *Feminist Criminology* 4, no. 1 (2009): 32–56.

Ewing, Walter. "The Legacy of Racism within the U.S. Border Patrol." *American Immigration Council*, February 10, 2021. www.americanimmigrationcouncil.org.

Executive Order. "Border Security and Immigration Enforcement Improvements." January 25, 2017. www.whitehouse.gov.

Freedom House. "Countries at the Crossroads Report, Honduras." April 8, 2010. https://freedomhouse.org.

Frelick, Bill, Ian M. Kysel, and Jennifer Podkul. "The Impact of Externalization of Migration Controls on the Rights of Asylum Seekers and Other Migrants." *Journal on Migration and Human Security* 4 (2016): 190–220.

Fry, Ralph, Dr. Roger Morgan, and Pete Melendez. *Cómo cambiar la conducta destructiva en los adolescentes*. Boulder City, Nevada: Parent Project, 2016.

Gelatt, Julia. "Explainer: How the U.S. Legal Immigration System Works." *Migration Policy Institute*, April 2019. www.migrationpolicy.org.

General Accounting Office. "Unaccompanied Children: HHS Can Take Further Actions to Monitor Their Care." February 5, 2016. http://www.gao.gov.

Ghandehari, Setareh, Bob Libal, and Priya Sreenivasen. "Broken Promises: Limits of Biden's Executive Order on Private Prisons." *Detention Watch Network, Project South*, December 2, 2021. http://detentionwatchnetwork.org.

Gilardi, Jasper. "Ally or Exploiter? The Smuggler-Migrant relationship is a Complex One." *Migration Policy Institute*, February 5, 2020. www.migrationpolicy.org.

Gilman, Denise. "The U.S. Deportation System is Verging on Lawlessness." *Guardian*, August 23, 2017. www.theguardian.com.

Glenn-Levin Rodriguez, Naomi. *Fragile Families: Foster Care, Immigration, and Citizenship*. Philadelphia, PA: University of Pennsylvania Press, 2017.

Gomberg-Muñoz, Ruth. *Becoming Legal: Immigration Law and Mixed-Status Families*. New York: Oxford University Press, 2017.

Gonzales, Roberto G. *Lives in Limbo: Undocumented and Coming of Age in America*. Oakland: University of California Press, 2016.

González, Yaatsil Guevara. "Navigating with Coyotes. Pathways of Central American Migrants in Mexico's Southern Border." *ANNALS of the American Academy of Political and Social Science* 676, no. 1 (2018): 174–93.

Harlan, Chico. "Inside the Administration's 1 billion Deal to Detain Central American Asylum Seekers." *Washington Post*, August 14, 2016. www.washingtonpost.com.

Hernández, Arelis R., Nick Miroff, and Maria Sacchetti. "46 Migrants Found Dead in Texas Inside Sweltering Tractor-Trailer." *Washington Post*, June 27, 2022. www.washingtonpost.com.

Hermannsdorfer, Claudia. "Declaration of Claudia Hermannsdorfer, Expert on Women's Rights in Honduras." April 29, 2020. https://supportkind.org.

Heyman, Josiah. "The US-Mexico Border since 2014: Overt Migration Contention and Normalized Violence." In *Handbook on Human Security, Borders and Migration*, 54–70. Cheltenham, UK: Edward Elgar, 2021.

Horton, Sarah, and Josiah Heyman, eds. *Paper Trails: Migrants, Documents, and Legal Insecurity*. Durham, NC: Duke University Press, 2020.

Human Rights Clinic at the University of Texas School of Law and Fray Juan de Larios Diocesan Human Rights Centre in Coahuila. "Control . . . Over the Entire State of Coahuila. An Analysis of Testimonies in Trials against Zeta Members in San Antonio, Austin, and Del Rio, Texas." November 2017. https://law.utexas.edu.

Human Rights Watch. "Closed Doors: Mexico's Failure to Protect Central American Refugee and Migrant Children." March 31, 2016. www.hrw.org.

———. "El Salvador Events of 2019." 2020. www.hrw.org.

———. "Guatemala Events of 2020." 2021. www.hrw.org.

Huttner, Sophie. "El Salvador's Femicide Crisis." *Yale Review of International Studies* (March 2020). http://yris.yira.org.

Immigration Legal Resource Center. "Unaccompanied Minors and New Executive Orders." March 21, 2017. www.ilrc.org.

Inter-American Commission on Human Rights. "Strategic Plan 2011–2015." *Organization of American States*, 2016. www.oas.org.

Jesuit Conference of Canada and the United States. "Intake without Oversight: Firsthand Experiences with the Customs and Border Protection Complaints Process." July, 2017. https://kinoborderinitiative.org.

Johnson, Jeh C. "Statement on Southwest Border Security." Department of Homeland Security, March 9, 2016. www.dhs.gov.

Kandal, William A. "Unaccompanied Alien Children: An Overview." *Congressional Research Service*, 2017. https://fas.org.

Kanstroom, Daniel, and M. Brinton Lykes, eds. *The New Deportations Delirium: Interdisciplinary Responses.* New York: New York University Press, 2015.

Kerwin, Donald, Mike Nicholson, Daniela Alulema, and Robert Warren. "U.S. Foreign-Born Essential Workers by Status and State and the Global Pandemic." *Center for Migration Studies* 8, no. 1 (2020): 282–300. https://doi:10.1177/2331502420952752.

Kids in Need of Defense. "Improving the Protection and Fair Treatment of Unaccompanied Children." September, 2016. https://supportkind.org.

Kids in Need of Defense and Latin American Working Group. "Sexual and Gender-Based Violence and Migration Fact Sheet." August 2018. https://supportkind.org.

Kinskey, Emily. "These Stories Tell the Harsh Realities of Working in an Overseas Factory." *International Women's Media Foundation* and *Buzzfeed News*, November 5, 2018. https://www.iwmf.org.

Klobucista, Claire, Amelia Cheatham, and Diana Roy. "The U.S. Immigration Debate." *Council on Foreign Relations*, August 3, 2022. https://www.cfr.org.

Lind, Dara. "'Immigrants Are Coming Over the Border to Kill You' Is the Only Speech Trump Knows How to Give." *Vox*, January 9, 2019. https://www.vox.com.

Lowenstein, Antony. "Private Prisons Are Cashing in on Refugees' Desperation." *New York Times*, February 25, 2016. www.nytimes.com.

Luiselli, Valeria. *The Lost Children Archive.* New York: 4th Estate, Alfred A. Knopf, 2020.

Manning, Stephen. "Ending Artesia." Accessed on January 28, 2015. https://innovation-lawlab.org.

Marcelo, Philip, and Gerald Herbert. "U.S. Migrant Detentions Soar Despite Biden's Campaign Promise." *Guardian*, August 5, 2021. www.theguardian.com.

Marks, Dana Leigh, "I'm an Immigration Judge. Here's How We Can Fix Our Courts." *Washington Post*, April 12, 2019. www.washingtonpost.com.

Martinez, Daniel E., Jeremy Slack, and Josiah Heyman. *Bordering on Criminal: The Routine Abuse of Migrants in the Removal System, Part I: Migrant Mistreatment While in U.S. Custody*, January, 2013. www.researchgate.net.

Matter of A-B. 27 I & N Dec. 316 (A.G. 2018).

Menjívar, Cecilia. "Family Reorganization in a Context of Legal Uncertainty: Guatemalan and Salvadoran Immigrants in the United States." *International Journal of Sociology* 32, no. 2 (Autumn 2006): 223–45.

———. *Enduring Violence: Ladina Women's Lives in Guatemala.* Oakland: University of California, 2011.

Menjívar, Cecilia, and Daniel Kanstroom, eds. *Constructing Immigrant "Illegality": Critiques, Experiences, and Responses*, New York: Cambridge University Press, 2013.

Menjívar, Cecilia, and Shannon Drysdal Walsh. "The Architecture of Feminicide: The State, Inequalities and Everyday Violence in Honduras." *Latin American Research Review* 52 (August 2017): 221–40. https://doi.org/10.25222/larr.73.

Miroff, Nick. "Biden Prepares Asylum Overhaul at Border, but Court Challenges Loom." *Washington Post*, May 27, 2022. www.washingtonpost.com.

MSNBC. "Former Border Patrol Agent 'Not Surprised' at Racist, Sexist Report." The Beat with Ari, July 2, 2019. www.msnbc.com.

Murphey, David. "Moving Beyond Trauma: Child Migrants and Refugees in the United States." *Child Trends*, September 7, 2016. https://childtrends.org.

Musallo, Karen, and Marcelle Rice. "The Implementation of the One-Year Bar to Asylum." *Hasting International and Comparative Law Review* 31 (2008): 693–720. http://repository.uchastings.edu.

Narea, Nicole. "Poll: Most Americans Support a Path to Citizenship for Undocumented Immigrants; Biden's Proposal to Legalize 10.5 Million Undocumented Immigrants is Popular—but Can He Achieve It?" *Vox*, February 4, 2021. www.vox.com.

Nazario, Sonia. "'Someone is Always trying to Kill You.' The United States Cannot Erect a Wall and Expect Women to Resign Themselves to Being Slaughtered." *New York Times*, April 7, 2019.

O'Donnell, Guillermo. "The Quality of Democracy: Why the Rule of Law Matters." *Journal of Democracy* 15, no. 4 (2004): 32–46.

Olivo, Antonio. "Tensions over Immigration Heat Up between Trump Administration and Virginia's Largest Jurisdiction." *Washington Post*, April 3, 2018. www.washingtonpost.com.

Palmer, Emily, and Kirk Semple. "Portrait of Corruption by Honduran President, but in Another Man's Trial," *New York Times*, March 24, 2021.

Partlow, Joshua. "Rights Groups Sue U.S. Government, Alleging It is Turning Away Asylum Applicants at Mexico Border." July 12, 2017, *Washington Post*. www.washingtonpost.com.

Ramos et al v. Wolf et al. United States Court of Appeals for the 9th Circuit, no. 18–1698, September 14, 2020.

Ranji-Nogales, Jay, Andrew Schoenholtz, and Philip Schrag. "Refugee Roulette: Disparities in Asylum Adjudication." *Stanford Law Review* 60 (2007): 295–412.

Redmon, Jeremy, and Lautaro Grinspan. "Exclusive: Ga. Immigration Facility to become One of the Nation's Largest." *Atlanta Journal Constitution*, February 4, 2022. https://ajc.com.

Roberts, Bryan, Gordon Hanson, Derekh Cornwell, and Scott Borger. "An Analysis of Migrant Smuggling Costs along the Southwest Border." Office of Immigration Statistics, Department of Homeland Security, November 2010. www.dhs.gov.

Rose, Joel and Scott Newman. "The Biden Administration is Fighting in Court to Keep a Trump Era Immigration Policy." *All Things Considered*, NPR, September 20, 2021. www.npr.org.

Sacchetti, Maria. "ICE Holds Growing Numbers of Immigrants at Private Facilities Despite Biden Campaign Promises to End Practice." *Washington Post*, December 1, 2021. www.washingtonpost.com.

Sacchetti, Maria, and Nick Miroff. "Border Patrol Agents Who Made Violent, Lewd Facebook Posts and Faced Flawed Disciplinary Action Process at CBP, House Investigation Finds." *Washington Post*, October 25, 2021. www.washingtonpost.com.

Sanchez, Gabriella, and Sheldon Zhang. "Rumors, Encounters, Collaborations and Survival: The Migrant Smuggling Drug Trafficking Nexus in the U.S. Southwest." *ANNALS of the American Academy of Political and Social Science* 676 (2018): 135–51.

Seelke, Clare Ribando. "El Salvador: Background and U.S. Relations." Congressional Research Service, July 1, 2020, R43616. www.crsreports.congress.gov.

Sessions, Jeff. "Zero-Tolerance Memorandum." Department of Justice, April 6, 2018. www.justice.gov.

Shear, Michael, Katie Benner, and Michael D. Schmidt. "'We Need to Take Away the Children,' No Matter How Young, Justice Department Officials Said." *New York Times*, October 7, 2020. www.nytimes.com.

Shire, Warsan. "Home." www.amnesty.ie.

Singh, Susheela, Elena Prada, and Edgar Kestler. "Induced Abortion and Unintended Pregnancy in Guatemala." *International Family Planning Perspectives* 32, no. 3 (2006): 136–45.

Slack, Jeremy. *Deported to Death: How Drug Violence is Changing Migration on the U.S.-Mexico Border*. Oakland: University of California Press, 2019.

Slack, Jeremy, and Howard Campbell. "On Narco-coyotaje: Illicit Regimes and Impacts on the U.S.-Mexico Border." *Antipodes* 48, no. 5 (2016): 1380–99.

Slavin, Denise Noonan, and Dana Leigh Marks. "You Be the Judge: Who Should Preside Over Immigration Cases, Where and How?" In *The New Deportation Delirium*, edited by Daniel Kanstroom and M. Brinton Lykes, 89–112. New York: New York University Press, 2015.

Soporoff, Jacob. *Separated: Inside an American Tragedy*. New York: Harper Collins, 2020.

Sorensen, Juliet, Alexandra Tarzikan, and Meredith Heim. "El Salvador's Abortion Ban Jails Women for Miscarriages and Stillbirths—Now One Woman's Family Seeks International Justice." *Conversation*, March 15, 2021. https://theconversation.com.

Stinchcomb, Dennis. *In Children's Best Interest. Charting a Child-Sensitive Approach to U.S. Immigration Policy*. CLALS Working Paper Series, no. 28. Washington, DC: American University, 2020.

Sullivan, Tim. "Denied Asylum Migrants Return to Place They Fear the Most: Home." *AP News*, December 29, 2019. https://apnews.com.

Tannen, Deborah. *Talking 9 to 5*. New York: William Morrow, 1994.

Terrio, Susan J. *Whose Child am I? Undocumented, Unaccompanied Children in U.S. Immigration Custody*. Oakland: University of California Press, 2015.

———. "The Curious Case of Jane Doe." In *Unaccompanied Migrant Children: Social, Legal and Ethical Perspectives*, edited by Hille Haker and Molly Greening, 101–20. Lanham, MD: Lexington Books, 2019.

———. "The Detention and Deportation of Minors in U.S. Immigration Custody." In *Life by Algorithms. How Roboprocesses are Remaking Our World*. Edited by Catherine L. Besteman and Hugh Gusterson, 59–76. Chicago: University of Chicago Press, 2019.

———. "Introduction. Encounters with Illegality." In *Illegal Encounters: The Effect of Detention and Deportation on Young People*, Deborah A. Boehm and Susan J. Terrio, 1–14. New York: New York University Press, 2019.

———. "Immigration Courts." In *Illegal Encounters. The Effect of Detention and Deportation on Young People*, edited by Deborah A. Boehm and Susan J. Terrio, 102–13. New York: New York University Press, 2019.

TRAC Immigration. "With the Immigration Court's Rocket Dockets Many Unrepresented Families Quickly Deported." October 18, 2016. https://trac.syr.edu.

———. "Asylum Success Varies Widely Among Immigration Judges." December 9, 2021. https://trac.syr.edu.

———. "Judge-by-Judge Asylum Decisions in Immigration Courts. FY 2016–2021." 2021. https://trac.syr.edu.

Trump, Donald J. "Address to the Nation on the Crisis at the Border." January 8, 2019. https://trumpwhitehouse.archives.gov.

United Nations High Commissioner on Refugees. "Women on the Run: First-Hand Accounts of Refugees Fleeing El Salvador, Guatemala, Honduras and Mexico." 2015. www.unhcr.org.

United States Citizenship and Immigration Services. "Humanitarian Petitions: U Visa Processing Times—Fiscal Year 2021 Report to Congress." August 2021. www.uscis.gov.

———. "Special Immigrant Services." November 2, 2022. www.uscis.gov.

US Customs and Border Protection. "CBP Releases May 2022: Monthly Operational Update." June 15, 2022. www.cbp.gov.

United States Department of State, Bureau of Democracy, Human Rights and Labor. "El Salvador 2014 Human Rights Report." Country Reports on Human Rights Practices for 2014. 2014. https://2009-2017.state.gov.

———. "Country Reports on Human Rights Practices: Honduras." March 31, 2020. https://www.state.gov.

United States Department of State, Bureau of Population, Refugees and Migration. "Report to Congress on Proposed Refugee Admissions for Fiscal Year 2021." 2020. www.state.gov.

Valdes, Marcela. "Their Lawsuit Prevented 400,000 deportations. Now It's Biden's Call." *New York Times Magazine*, April 11, 2021. www.nytimes.com.

Vargas, Antonio. "My Life as an Undocumented Immigrant." *New York Times Magazine*, June 26, 2011. www.nytimes.com.

Villaviciencio, Karla Cornejo. *The Undocumented Americans*. New York: One World, 2020.

———. "Waking Up from the American Dream. Growing Up Undocumented, I Learned that the Price of My Innocence Was the Guilt of My Parents." *New Yorker*, January 25, 2021. www.newyorker.com.

Violence Observatory of National Autonomous University of Honduras. 2020. https://www.state.gov/reports/2020-country-reports-on-human-rights-practices/honduras.

Vogt, Wendy. "Stuck in the Middle with You: The Intimate Labours of Mobility and Smuggling along Mexico's Migrant Route." *Geopolitics* 21, no. 2 (2016): 366–86.

Vogt, Wendy A. *Lives in Transit. Violence and Intimacy on the Migrant Journey*. Oakland: University of California Press, 2018.

Walsh, Shannon Drysdale, and Cecilia Menjívar. "Impunity and Multisided Violence in the Lives of Latin American Women: El Salvador in Comparative Perspective." *Current Sociology* 64, no. 4 (2016): 586–602.

Women's Refugee Commission. "Forced from Home: The Lost Boys and Girls of Central America." October 12, 2012. https://womensrefugeecommission.org.

———. "Prison for Survivors: The Detention of Women Seeking Asylum in the U.S." October 1, 2017. https://womensrefugeecommission.org.

———. "Chaos, Confusion, and Danger: The Remain in Mexico Program in El Paso." May 16, 2019. https://womensrefugeecommission.org.

Women's Refugee Commission, Lutheran Immigration Service, and Kids in Need of Defense. "Betraying Family Values. How U.S. Immigration Policy at the Border is Separating Families." February 12, 2017. https://www.womensrefugeecommission.org.

White House Press Office. "Fact Sheet." November 20, 2014. https://obamawhitehouse.archives.gov.

Yarris, Kristin. *Care Across Generations: Solidarity and Sacrifice in Transnational Families*. Stanford: Stanford University Press, 2017.

Zawodny, David. "An Immigration Courts Backlog Keeps Central American Youth in Legal Limbo." *North American Congress on Latin America*, June 29, 2021. https://nacla.org.

Zhang, Sheldon X., Gabriella E. Sanchez, and Luigi Achilli. "Crimes of Solidarity in Mobility: Alternative Views on Migrant Smuggling." *ANNALS of the American Academy of Political and Social Science*, 676, no. 1 (2018): 6–15.

INDEX

Abbott, Greg (Texas Governor): acknowledged link with shooter at the Walmart in El Paso, 171; expenditures on action against migrants, 171

Arpaio, Joe (former Maricopa County Sheriff): dehumanization of migrants, 171

Artesia (New Mexico) detention facility, 179n10; closed on 15 December 2014, 71; labeled a "deportation mill," 71; opened on 27 June 2014, 71

asylum: credible fear screening, 2, 6; aftermath of passing a credible fear interview, 11; hearings scheduled years in advance, 167; officer rule in, 166. *See also* Biden, Joseph R., Jr.; Garland, Merrick; Sessions, Jeff; Trump, Donald J.

Ayuda Social Services, 178n7; based in D.C., 39; provided legal assistance to Ines and daughter Isela, 39

Berks County Detention Center (Pennsylvania), 6; detention of families at, 5

Biden, Joseph R., Jr. (President), 177n4, 178n19, 178n17, 182n11; campaign promise to end for-profit detention, 163; El Salvador included in nations covered by Temporary Protected Status (TPS), 88; expansion of detention, 163; migrants expelled, 5; migrant protections under the Special Immigrant Juvenile Status (SIJS), 42; modification of asylum rules, 166; raised refugee admissions, 5, 168; removal of migrants, 5; reversal of Trump, Donald J. (President) migration policies, 5, 163; Temporary Protected Status (TPS) nations expanded, 88

Boehm, Debbie, 173–74, 176

Border Patrol, 64, 180n7 chap. 6, 182n16; abuse of children by, 97; assistance to migrant, 84; Congressional investigation of, 169–70; culture of institutional racism in, 96, 169; direct violence by, 97, 169; forms of violence in, 96, 129; officer misconduct not commonly punished, 170; operates with a degree of impunity, 96, 169–70; report on officer misconduct, 170; rescue of migrants, 1; training of agents, 96; use of the term "tonk," 96

Central America: characteristics of female migrants, 3; dislike for migrants from, 13; exodus from 3; high level of unaccompanied minors from, 91; majority of migrants after 2013, 3; people emigrate because of extreme poverty and violence in, 51; politicians enrich themselves but do not help residents, 51; threat of migrants from, 13; women first fled within home country, 3. *See also* El Salvador; Guatemala; Honduras

Charlton County (Georgia): bed capacity of 3,018, 164; operated by GEO Group, 164

Citizenship and Immigration Services (CIS), 26, 27, 39, 40. *See also* Special Immigrant Juvenile Status (SIJS)

ABOUT THE AUTHOR

SUSAN J. TERRIO is Professor Emerita of Anthropology and French Studies at Georgetown University. She is the author of *Whose Child Am I? Unaccompanied, Undocumented Children in U.S. Immigration Custody* and the co-editor of *Illegal Encounters: The Effect of Detention and Deportation on Young People.*

www.ingramcontent.com/pod-product-compliance
Lightning Source LLC
Chambersburg PA
CBHW020540030426
42337CB00013B/919